Security Management for Healthcare

Proactive Event Prevention and Effective Resolution

Security Management for Healthcare

Proactive Event Prevention
and Effective Resolution

By

Bernard J. Scaglione

A PRODUCTIVITY PRESS BOOK

First edition published in 2019
by Routledge/Productivity Press
52 Vanderbilt Avenue, 11th Floor New York, NY 10017
2 Park Square, Milton Park, Abingdon, Oxon OX14 4RN, UK

International Standard Book Number-13: 978-0-367-08680-0 (Hardback)
International Standard Book Number-13: 978-0-367-08677-0 (Paperback)
International Standard Book Number-13: 978-0-429-02370-5 (eBook)

Visit the Taylor & Francis Web site at
http://www.taylorandfrancis.com

Contents

Acknowledgement

During my career, I have come across many people that have influenced my life in a positive way. For me, the influences that impacted me the most were those individuals that stressed education and the pursuit of learning: using knowledge to continuously improve the quality of life and career. This pursuit for knowledge focused on not only education but learning from others, respecting other people for who they are and understanding that every individual is unique, and understanding that every person provides their own distinctive set of knowledge and skills developed through life. The first person in my life that helped me recognize the importance of education and knowledge was my mom, the woman who recently, at the age of 88, was admitted into college to pursue her doctorate degree. Growing up, she was able to balance her life, raising three kids, manage the household and attend college on a part time basis. She was able to obtain her bachelor's and master's degrees while I was growing up. Thanks, mom, for being you and allowing me to understand the importance of education and knowledge. As my career advanced, I have had the distinct pleasure to know and work with a man whose persistence and mentoring led to this book, a man whose forward thinking and understanding of the security field broadened my knowledge and experience. Thank you, Charlie Schnabolk, for your mentoring and knowledge throughout my career. Lastly, I need to thank my wife of 33 years, who I have known for 43 years and who has certainly been a major influence in my life and career, providing advice and being a partner in life and career. This book is dedicated to the three individuals that have influenced my life and career the most. Thank you all for your advice, support and guidance.

Introduction

The beginning of the 21st century has brought many challenges to health-care security, from the possibility of a terrorist attack to pandemic flu, work-place violence including an active shooter, strict legislative requirements, and continued financial constraints. Moving forward, healthcare security executives will need to have a better understanding of legislative require-ments. Monies previously available for staffing and technology will shrink. Healthcare security professionals will need to manage staff and resources differently, increasing service levels while reducing costs. This will require security executives to be more data driven and to look at alternatives to tra-ditional methods of supplying security services.

In today's terrorist-conscious society hospitals need to address access restriction—identifying all persons entering their facilities and controlling access to high-risk areas like the emergency department and infrastructure portals. In 2003, the Office of Homeland Security (OHS) published "The National Strategy for the Physical Protection of Critical Infrastructures and Key Assets." This publication identified hospitals as the primary caretaker of emergency service personnel and injured attack victims, as well as providing medical services to their surrounding community. Moreover, the report high-lighted the need for formulating protective strategies to prevent contamina-tion from biological, chemical, and radiological agents; theft of toxic agents; and possible sabotage of the hospital's infrastructure.

In response to potential catastrophic events, hospitals need to control access to prevent contamination. Entrances that have historically never been secured now need to be lockable. In emergencies, hospital security must stop all persons wishing to gain entry so that they can screen for biological, chemical, and radiological contaminants. Security staff must be trained to identify basic toxic agents, and hospital staff must provide decontamination services to patients and emergency service workers before they enter the emergency room for medical treatment.

The 21st century will see many new, challenging diseases, along with the resurfacing of older, nearly extinct ones. Hospital staff must be trained to immediately recognize symptoms from these illnesses. Security staff must be more aware of possible exposures from persons on the street walking into the hospital or clinic and of course the emergency room. The recent epidemics of SARS, H1N1, and Ebola have demonstrated the reality of this challenge, clearly illustrating our need for continued training and education of security staff when it comes to the handling of high-risk communicable diseases.

The federal government and other compliance organizations continue to regulate healthcare security organizations. The Joint Commission (TJC) requires the maintenance of a security plan, an annual assessment of risk, the identification of "security-sensitive" areas, and the annual assessment of performance. The Centers for Medicare & Medicaid Services (CMS) ensures a safe environment for all patients. The CMS regulates how and when patient restraints are used and how they are applied. It looks closely at the weapons that security departments utilize in the arrest and/or restraint of patients who cause physical harm to staff, visitors, or other patients. The Nuclear Regulatory Commission (NRC) requires the responsible storage and transport of nuclear and radioactive materials utilized in the treatment of patients. These radioactive sources are considered a terrorist risk and must be properly secured and monitored. The National Center for Missing and Exploited Children (NCMEC) publishes recommendations on the protection of infants and children housed or visiting in healthcare institutions. The NCMEC recommends the development, testing, and critique of a proactive written prevention plan. The Occupational Safety and Health Administration (OSHA) provides guidelines in the areas of workplace violence and employee identification. In 2014, OSHA published a revised version of "Guidelines for Preventing Workplace Violence for Health Care and Social Service Workers." This document concluded that healthcare workers had the highest incidence of assault compared with all other professions outside of healthcare. Moreover, the study recommends that hospitals and other health-related organizations implement physical security measures to reduce verbal and physical assaults. Violence will most likely increase during the 21st century. Specifically, increases will occur in domestic violence, elder abuse, gangs, and gun crimes. Many hospitals have delegated these antiviolence initiatives to the security department. Security personnel must be taught to properly respond to disruptive patients, visitors, and staff, and trained to verbally de-escalate and physically restrain individuals who become verbally threatening or physically abusive. The Health Insurance Portability and Accountability Act (HIPAA) enhances the protection of patients' medical information. In February 2003, hospitals were required to provide physical security controls for medical information and implement policies to restrict and monitor the distribution and release of medical information. At many healthcare institutions, this responsibility has fallen upon security, who have been asked to install access control technologies in medical record departments and medical record storage environments, as well as conduct training programs and monitor policy compliance. Lastly, the "red flags rule" requires creditors to have identity theft prevention programs in place that will identify, detect, and respond to patterns, practices, or specific activities that point to the identity theft of patient medical records and related information. In 2009, the American Recovery and Reinvestment Act was signed into law. This law requires the use of electronic health records (EHRs) by physicians and hospitals. This portion of the bill is called the Health Information Technology for Economic and Clinical Health Act, or the HITECH Act. Included in the bill are requirements for the physical and virtual securing of medical information.

Security departments in the new millennium will face increased financial restraints due in large part to changes in the economy and state and federal legislation. Political pressure will force reimbursement to decline while the cost of providing healthcare will increase. To meet the challenge of shrinking security dollars, security must rely on alternative or more innovative methods for providing services. The use of CCTV, access control, and physical security applications will be far more important as we proceed further into the new millennium. Security administrators will need to be more knowledgeable of security technology and products. Beyond the expanded utilization of security-related technologies, security executives must change their mindset from reactive to a more proactive model of detecting crimes before they occur. This will require a system of evaluation designed so that the actual effect of the security program can be measured.

Security staff will deal increasingly more with different and diverse cultures, many of which staff may not understand, leading to confrontations or a reluctance to interact. Training related to the different cultures and their customs will need to be ongoing. Hospital security will also need to hire a more diverse group of security officers. Having security staff that can relate to the population they serve will help them better deal with a more diverse population.

This book offers a proactive, advanced look at healthcare security. It provides tools and processes to help administer security services that will meet the challenges of 21st-century healthcare security needs, as well as the future, ever-changing environment of healthcare security.[1]

Reference

1. Scaglione, Bernard J. and Luizzo, Anthony J. Hospital security in the 21st century: What should we expect. *Journal of Healthcare Protection Management*, Vol. 22, No. 1, pp. 75–80. 2006.

Chapter 1

Regulatory Compliance

Introduction

Regulations within the healthcare field are increasing. More and more federal, state, and local agencies are developing rules and regulations for the healthcare industry. Complying with regulatory agencies is a very important part of managing security in the healthcare arena. Several federal and state agencies influence security services within the healthcare environment. In order to comply with healthcare security regulations, it is important to understand the rules and regulations created by each regulatory agency and the meaning behind the regulations that they enforce. A firm understanding of all regulations that involve security can help us to run an effective and efficient security program.

Joint Commission on Accreditation of Healthcare Organizations (The Joint Commission)

The Joint Commission is a nonprofit organization that has accredited thousands of healthcare organizations and programs in the United States. A majority of state governments recognize Joint Commission accreditation as a condition of licensure for the receipt of Medicaid and Medicare reimbursements. The Joint Commission was formerly the Joint Commission on Accreditation of Healthcare Organizations (JCAHO), and previous to that the Joint Commission on Accreditation of Hospitals (JCAH).

In 1951, the Joint Commission on Accreditation of Hospitals was created by merging the Hospital Standardization Program with similar programs run by the American College of Physicians, the American Hospital Association, the American Medical Association, and the Canadian Medical Association. The JCAH was renamed the Joint Commission on Accreditation of Hospitals in 1951, but it was not until 1965, when the federal government decided that a hospital meeting Joint Commission accreditation met the Medicare Conditions of Participation, that accreditation had any official impact. However, Section 125 of the Medicare Improvements for Patients and Providers Act of 2008 (MIPPA) removed the Joint Commission's statutorily guaranteed accreditation authority for hospitals, effective July 15, 2010. At that time, the Joint Commission's hospital accreditation program would be subject to Centers for Medicare & Medicaid Services (CMS) requirements for organizations seeking accrediting authority. In 1987, the company was renamed the Joint Commission on Accreditation of Healthcare Organizations (JCAHO; pronounced "Jay-co"). In 2007, the Joint Commission on Accreditation of Healthcare Organizations underwent a major rebranding and simplified its name to the "The Joint Commission."

Hospitals voluntarily seek accreditation by paying the Joint Commission to conduct a self-policing survey once every three years. Joint Commission accreditation is tied directly to a hospital's Medicaid and Medicare funding. Originally, Joint Commission accreditation was provided on a percentage scale, but due to complaints in the rating system it was changed to "pass-fail" in 2005. In 2006, the Joint Commission changed from scheduled to unannounced surveys.

A typical survey team consists of a hospital administrator, a registered nurse, a medical practice specialist or doctor, and an ambulatory care specialist or a life safety specialist. Each surveyor has a specific role during the survey, but as a team, their role is to evaluate all of the standards created by the Joint Commission. The Joint Commission uses the "tracer" methodology to conduct its surveys. The tracer method selects a patient, resident, or client's medical record as a roadmap to move through the hospital in order to assess and evaluate the organization's compliance with Joint Commission standards. Surveyors retrace the care process through observation and dialogue with the staff that cared for the chosen patient. Their focus during the survey is to determine trends or patterns that point to system-level issues within the hospital's safety and quality of care.

The Joint Commission survey is not just observational; it also provides opportunities to educate staff and leaders on proper care, as well as to share best practices from other healthcare organizations surveyed. The Joint Commission revises its Environment of Care Standards each year. It is a good practice for security to review standards on a yearly basis to ensure that no new standards have been created or current ones revised. The basic structure of the security standards requires an operational plan and data collection in order to analyze and continuously improve the security services provided to the hospital and its patients, visitors, and staff.

Sentinel Event

The Joint Commission started a program in 1996 to improve patient care by collecting and sharing knowledge and statistics on adverse events occurring within the organizations it accredited. Called a "sentinel event," each hospital organization is required to report unexpected occurrences, such as accidental death, serious physical or psychological injury, and infant abduction. The hospital completes an in-depth analysis to determine what caused the event and how the event can be prevented in the future. An adverse or undesirable event includes patient falls, medication errors, procedural errors/complications, completed suicidal behavior, and missing patient events. The Joint Commission has also requested that healthcare members investigate "near misses." A near miss is a situation that could have resulted in an accident, injury, or illness but did not. An example of a near miss would be a surgical or other procedure almost performed on the wrong patient due to lapses in verification of patient identification but caught at the last minute.

Root Cause Analysis

The Joint Commission expects organizations to conduct a full investigation into why the adverse event occurred and determine what can be done to prevent it from recurring. The process that the Joint Commission utilizes for the investigation and prevention of adverse events is called "root cause analysis." Root cause analysis is a process for identifying the basic or contributing factors that contribute to variations in performance. A root cause analysis focuses primarily on systems and processes, not individual performances.

Root cause analysis is not about blame or negligence; it is about finding methods or processes to improve the situation in order to prevent its recurrence. Security may be involved in a root cause analysis when an event involves a process that security is part of, for example, an infant abduction or patient elopement.

Process Improvement

The Joint Commission requires hospitals to collect information to monitor conditions in the hospital environment and improve security program processes. This information or data is collected in order to manage risk, risks that are identified by the security department through internal sources such as ongoing monitoring of the Environment of Care, results of root cause analyses, and results of annual risk assessments. External sources such as sentinel event alerts, trade publications, and local, state, and national news events. The collection process must include the continued monitoring, reporting, and investigating of security-related incidents that involve patients, staff, visitors, and volunteers, as well as the analysis and trending of collected data on potential high-risk incidents. The collection of data should include a yearly assessment of risk within the hospital and the identification of high-risk areas or what the Joint Commission calls "security-sensitive areas." The security department should use the results of data analysis to identify opportunities to resolve security issues and minimize or eliminate the identified security risks. As part of the analysis process, the security department must develop and monitor what are called performance indicators. These are data metrics developed from the collection and analysis of security-related data. The resulting data analysis should be used to measure improvement in security issues and risks.[1]

Security Management Plan

The Joint Commission requires all hospitals to development and implement a written "security management plan." The plan should describe how the organization establishes and maintains a program that protects staff, patients, and visitors. The plan should designate those persons responsible for developing, implementing, and monitoring the plan and address all of the Joint Commission standards within the plan. For example, the plan should outline, but not detail, the controlling of access to and from sensitive areas or how the security department will provide for vehicular access to the emergency department. The plan should be written in plain English and outline the activities and actions of the security department, including its mission statement and department values. Many hospitals write their security plan by recording the individual standards and then describing the processes that the hospital uses to meet each standard. This is the best technique in writing the plan. The Joint Commission prefers this type of written plan because a surveyor can easily review the plan and see how the plan meets the standards. The security management plan should be reviewed annually when the new standards are published. This will keep the plan up to date and allow the security department to stay in compliance with the Joint Commission while modifying operations and processes as necessary to meet standards.

Training Competencies

The Joint Commission wants security departments to evaluate staff performance based on their job responsibilities and training. This evaluation should be conducted at least yearly or as necessary to ensure the highest level of staff performance. This evaluation should be documented and completed especially where job functions involve direct patient care. For security, that means competence in patient restraint, patient watches, customer service, and any other job functions that relate to patient care. The Joint Commission requires that this assessment method utilize competencies in skills that are necessary to perform security officer work. Competency methods include test taking, demonstration/observation, and the use of simulation. Staff competence should start at orientation and be utilized through all training conducted with the security staff for their entire career. Competency assessments should be documented and stored in each employee's personnel file. When a staff member's competence does not meet expectations, the Joint Commission wants hospitals to document corrective actions. For example, job functions for each security post or job should be broken down to the essential job components. For officers that stand in the main entrance, competencies may include where the officer stands, what he says to greet patients and visitors, or the checking of employee IDs or visitor passes. Failing a competency evaluation means the security department should provide documented additional training and reassessment to ensure that the officer meets the competency.

Security Education

The Joint Commission requires that all hospital staff be oriented and educated about the security processes within their area of work and that they possess the knowledge and skill required to perform their responsibilities under the security management plan. The standard requires that personnel be able to describe or demonstrate knowledge of security risks, like infant abduction and reporting procedures for security incidents involving patients, visitors, personnel, and property. Under the Human Resource Standard, hospital personnel that work in designated security-sensitive areas should be able to describe or demonstrate the security risks associated with their area, how to minimize them, emergency procedures for security incidents, and the reporting procedures for security incidents specific to their area. Many hospital security departments use new employee orientation and annual in-service training to review security policy and practices with staff. Many hospitals include procedures like workplace violence, active shooter, and escort services and basic crime prevention information in their security orientation and annual in-service training.

Forensic Personnel

Training under the Joint Commission includes training community personnel that visit or stay within the hospital. Published within the Human Resource Standard, most hospitals require security to provide training to and act as a liaison with law enforcement personnel while on hospital property. The Joint Commission wants law enforcement personnel to be oriented on hospital and security procedures. Procedures like fire response, smoking, and patient restraint should all be taught to law enforcement personnel who are in the hospital for prisoner security or treatment escort. Because of a number of events that have occurred in healthcare facilities with law enforcement personnel and their prisoner patients, the Joint Commission requires the education of law enforcement personnel that are present in a healthcare facility. This standard includes law enforcement personnel who are guarding an inpatient who is a prisoner or who visit the hospital facility on a regular basis and are present within the facility for an extended period guarding outpatient prisoners. The standard requires that these law enforcement personnel be educated on hospital policy and procedure that may affect them during their time within the hospital. Law enforcement personnel need to be educated on basic safety protocols like fire response and patient restraint, visiting hours, the smoking policy, and the procedure for emergent medical situations like a heart attack. The standard requires the creation and mainte- nance of a logbook documenting training sessions. Security must document law enforcement personnel training and provide some written educational material to law enforcement personnel. Many hospitals place all of the required information on a laminated card that fits into the officer's memo book. This way the law enforcement officer has immediate access to the information when needed. Some hospital security departments attend local law enforcement roll calls and provide the necessary information annually.

Emergency Preparedness

Hospitals must have a written emergency management plan in place that includes security. The plan requires advance preparation to support security during an emergency and describes the response procedures to follow when emergencies occur. The plan must coordinate its security activities and uti- lize an "all-hazards" approach that is flexible enough to address the duration, scale, and cause of a specific emergency. The plan should identify security's capability and response procedures during a disaster and coordinate security activities with community agencies when those services are available. The plan should include procedures to control or close entrances into and out of the healthcare facility and control movement of individuals and vehicles within the healthcare facility.

Security Officer Licensure

Many states require security staff to be licensed. Whether in-house or a contract service, the Joint Commission requires all licensed personnel that come in any sort of contact with patients to have an active license while working. The hospital must be able to verify that a working employee has an active license, one that has not expired or been suspended. To ensure a license is active, the Joint Commission requires primary source verification of licensure. Primary source verification is verification of an active license from the original source to determine the accuracy of the qualifications and license status. The hospital, or security department, must have a process in place that will provide primary source verification. A copy of each security officer's license must be placed within their employment folder and be available during a survey. Proof of the verification process may need to be demonstrated as part of a survey.

Centers for Medicare & Medicaid Services

The Centers for Medicare & Medicaid Services (CMS) is the administrator of Medicare and Medicaid health insurance along with other related quality assurance programs. The CMS maintains compliance to Medicare and Medicaid institutions by providing health and safety standards for laboratories, acute and continuing care providers like hospitals, nursing homes, home health agencies, hospices, and other facilities that accept Medicare and Medicaid insurance. President Lyndon B. Johnson signed the Social Security Amendments into law on July 30, 1965, establishing Medicare and Medicaid. The Social Security Administration (SSA) became responsible for administering Medicare. The Social and Rehabilitation Service (SRS) became responsible for the administration of Medicaid. Both agencies were then combined under the Department of Health, Education, and Welfare (HEW). In 1977, the Health Care Financing Administration (HCFA) was established and became responsible for the coordination of Medicare and Medicaid under the Department of Health and Human Services (HHS). Medicare was implemented in 1966 with the purpose of extending health coverage to Americans aged 65 or older, only half of whom had insurance at the time. Medicaid provided healthcare for low-income children, the elderly, the blind, and individuals with other disabilities. In 1972, Medicare was extended to cover people under 65 with permanent disabilities, and Medicaid eligibility for elderly, blind, and disabled residents under state care was linked to eligibility for the newly enacted federal Supplemental Security Income (SSI) program. The Medicare Catastrophic Coverage Act of 1988 included the most significant changes since the enactment of Medicare, including improved hospital and skilled nursing facility benefits, mammography coverage, outpatient prescription drug benefits, and limits on patient liability. The act was repealed a year later in response to protests from higher-income elderly over new premiums, and charge-based payments were replaced with a new service fee schedule. In 2003, the Medicare Prescription Drug, Improvement, and Modernization Act (MMA) introduced the most significant changes in the history of the program, creating a stand-alone prescription drug option and significantly enhancing the presence and authority of private providers. The Medicare and Medicaid law resides under 42 Code of Federal Regulations (CFR) 483.400, Title 42—Public Health, Chapter IV—Centers for Medicare & Medicaid Services, Department of Health and Human Services. Under the law, the secretary of Health and Human Services has the authority to approve, disapprove, or terminate Medicare participation to providers and suppliers if they do not meet all conditions and requirements resulting from a survey or inspection. The secretary gives CMS the authority for ensuring that healthcare providers and suppliers, participating in Medicare and Medicaid, meet all federal health-care requirements. If conditions are not met, CMS can either undertake an action to terminate benefits or apply one or more of the remedies specified in the act.

Survey Inspection

The enforcement of CMS regulations is conducted through the performance of on-site surveys. State agencies are authorized to set and enforce standards for Medicaid. Enforcement includes the ability to perform surveys to support its certifications. Depending on the state, the state health department usually conducts the CMS survey process. Surveys are implemented when an adverse incident occurs within a facility or the state health department gets a formal complaint from a patient or staff member. The focus of the survey is to determine whether a provider meets the requirements for participation in the Medicare and/or Medicaid program through evaluation of the CMS regulations. It is CMS policy to have unannounced surveys for all providers. Sections of the act allow nongovernmental institutions to accredit hospitals for CMS. Currently, these include the Joint Commission on Accreditation of Healthcare Organizations (JCAHO), Det Norske Veritas (DNV), and the American Osteopathic Association (AOA).

Use of Restrictive Devices

The CMS dictates the use of handcuffs or other restrictive devices on patients. CMS regulations state that law enforcement officials can use restrictive devices for custody, detention, and public safety reasons but not for any provisions related to the care of a patient. That means handcuffs, shackles, waist chains, or flex cuffs can only be used on a prisoner for security purposes, to ensure the safety of the officer and the healthcare staff. Security personnel are included in this provision. Security personnel cannot use handcuffs or any other law enforcement–type restraint during the care of a patient, for example, using handcuffs on a patient with behavioral health issues or Alzheimer's disease who wishes to leave the hospital, or restraining a patient with handcuffs or shackles who is physically out of control or violent. In these situations, patients must be restrained based on hospital policy utilizing leather restraints, Velcro restraints, or a chemical restraint. No handcuffs or shackles can be used to gain control of the patient in these situations. Some hospitals will allow the use of handcuffs by security officers to temporarily gain control of an out-of-control patient or violent patient. Before utilizing handcuffs or other law enforcement–type devices for temporary restraint of patients, the hospital legal and risk management departments should be consulted to see if it is a process that does not violate the CMS standard.

Abuse or Harassment

CMS states that patients have the right to be free from all forms of abuse or harassment. This rule prohibits all forms of abuse, neglect, and harassment, whether from staff, other patients, or visitors. CMS defines abuse as the willful infliction of injury, unreasonable confinement, intimidation, or punishment, with resulting physical harm, pain, or mental anguish. This includes staff neglect or indifference to infliction of injury or intimidation of one patient by another. Healthcare institutions must have policies and processes in place that ensure patients are free of all forms of abuse, neglect, or harassment. This includes assurance that staff are properly screened before employment for records of abuse or neglect and that they are not hired or retained if they have such records. The healthcare organization must also implement a proactive approach to identify and correct all incidents and occurrences that constitute or contribute to abuse and neglect.

Behavioral Health

The Centers for Medicare & Medicaid Services has adopted "Conditions of Participation for Intermediate Care Facilities for the Mentally Retarded." This section outlines the care and restraint of patients. Seclusion or restraint must only be used when less restrictive interventions have been determined to be ineffective in protecting the patient, staff members, and others from violence or harm. Restraint or seclusion is only to be used to ensure the immediate physical safety of the patient, staff, or others. In most hospitals, security plays a role in patient restraint and seclusion, so it is important that security directors understand this section of the CMS standard.

CMS defines seclusion as the involuntary confinement of a patient alone in a room or area where the patient is physically prevented from leaving. According to CMS, seclusion can only be used for the management of violent or self-destructive behavior. Restraint is defined as any manual method, physical or mechanical device, material, or equipment that immobilizes or reduces the ability of a patient to move his or her arms, legs, body, or head freely. A drug is considered a restraint when it is used to manage the patient's behavior or restrict the patient's freedom of movement. CMS recommends that any form of seclusion and/or restraint be discontinued at the earliest possible time, utilizing them only as a last resort. Within one hour of seclusion or restraint, the patient must be evaluated face-to-face by a physician or other licensed independent practitioner or by a registered nurse or physician assistant who has met specified training requirements. These training requirements are outlined in the CMS standard.[2]

The CMS believes that all patients have the right to be free from restraint or seclusion, of any form, imposed as a means of coercion, discipline, convenience, or retaliation by staff. Public scrutiny of restraint and seclusion is increasing, and legal standards are changing, consistent with growing evidence that the use of these interventions is dangerous and can be avoided. Minimizing the use of restraints reduces the risk of tragedy, negative media coverage, or legal judgments. For security, depending on the role that security plays in the restraint process, both the CMS and Joint Commission recommend that all security staff that have the potential to touch a patient during a restraint obtain training in crisis intervention. The training should include verbal de-escalation techniques, self-defense, patient takedown, and application of restraints. This training should be conducted annually, with competencies, and a clinician who is familiar with the restraint application process should teach the application of restraints. During a CMS or Joint Commission survey, a surveyor has the right to ask for training records to ensure that security personnel are provided with annual crisis intervention and restraint application training.

Patient Safety

Although security is not specifically mentioned in CMS regulations, the CMS provides patients with the right to receive care in a safe environment—an environment that a reasonable person would consider to be safe. This means the protection of vulnerable patients, including newborns and children, and the review and analysis of patient and staff incident and accident reports to identify any incidents or patterns of incidents that do not provide a safe environment. During a CMS survey, the security program can be reviewed—the security management plan and all policies and procedures related to access control, emergency preparedness, or any other procedures deemed important as part of the survey. Policies and procedures related to patient restraint, the use of handcuffs, and other weapons can be reviewed by the CMS during a survey as well. This includes officer training, competencies, and licensure. Most importantly, the infant and child protection plan can be reviewed, along with drills and all policies and procedures.[3]

Health Insurance Portability and Accountability Act

The Health Insurance Portability and Accountability Act of 1996 (HIPAA) was adopted by Congress in order to provide privacy protection for individual health information. With advances in electronic technology, Congress felt that electronic health information could erode the privacy of health records. HIPAA is administered by the Department of Health and Human Services, which is required to adopt standards for electronic healthcare transactions and code sets, unique health identifiers, and health record security. This included a mandate to adopt federal privacy protections for individually identifiable health information. The HIPAA Privacy Rule, published in December 2000 and modified in August 2002, set standards for the protection of individually identifiable health information from three healthcare entities: health plans, healthcare clearinghouses, and healthcare providers who conduct standard healthcare transactions electronically. The Department of Health and Human Services published a final Security Rule in February 2003. This rule sets national standards for protecting the confidentiality, integrity, and availability of electronic protected health information. In January 2013, the HHS issued the Omnibus Rule, or HITECH Act, which expanded HIPAA requirements and penalties for the misuse or improper disclosure of health information. The Office for Civil Rights is responsible for enforcing the HIPAA Security Rule and the confidentiality provisions of the Patient Safety Rule. The Centers for Medicare & Medicaid Services enforces rules laid out for the Transactions and Code Sets Standards, Employer Identifier Standard, and National Provider Identifier Standard. All of the HIPAA rules are located under the federal administrative code at 45 CFR Parts 160, 162, and 164.[4]

Protected health information (PHI) is defined as all individually identifiable health information held or transmitted by a hospital and its business associate, in any form or media. Individually identifiable health information includes demographic data specific to:

■ The individual's past, present, or future physical or mental health or condition
■ The provision of healthcare to the individual
■ The past, present, or future payment for the provision of healthcare to the individual
■ The identification of an individual by common identifiers, like name, address, birth date, or Social Security number

Under HIPAA, hospitals and healthcare institutions must develop and implement written privacy policies and procedures and designate a privacy official responsible for:

■ Developing and implementing HIPAA policies and procedures
■ Receiving complaints
■ Providing individuals with information on privacy practices

All healthcare institutions must have procedures in place to accept and handle individual complains about compliance and identify how complaints are handled within the healthcare institution. Healthcare organizations must train all staff on privacy policies and procedures. This includes employees, volunteers, and trainees, and may include other persons whose conduct is outlined in the HIPAA provisions. Healthcare organizations must maintain, for at least six years, its privacy policies and procedures, privacy practice notices, disposition of complaints, and other actions, activities, and designations related to the Privacy Rule.

Hospitals must maintain reasonable and appropriate administrative, technical, and physical safeguards to prevent intentional or unintentional use or disclosure of protected health information, for example, shredding protected health information documents before discarding them, securing medical records with lock and key, and limiting access to keys. HIPAA defines administrative safeguards as "administrative actions, and policies and procedures, to manage the selection, development, implementation, and maintenance of security measures to protect electronic protected health information and to manage the conduct of the covered entity's workforce in relation to the protection of that information." Compliance with the Administrative Safeguards Standard requires an evaluation of the security controls already in place, an accurate and thorough risk analysis, and a series of documented solutions unique to the hospital.[2]

There is a provision of HIPAA that is important to healthcare security professionals. This rule is designed to balance the protection of the individual with the importance of law enforcement functions. Under specific situations, HIPAA permits the disclosure of PHI to law enforcement officials, without the patient's written authorization. Most common is the release of medical information through a court order or court-ordered warrant, subpoena, or summons issued by a judicial officer or a grand jury. Release by administrative request, such as an administrative subpoena or investigative demand, or other written request from a law enforcement official. This rule requires all administrative requests to include or be accompanied by a written statement that the information requested is relevant and material, specific and limited in scope.

Healthcare organizations can release information to law enforcement requesting PHI for the purposes of identifying or locating a suspect, fugitive, material witness, or missing person. This information is limited to:

■ Name and address
■ Date and place of birth
■ Social security number
■ ABO blood type and Rh factor
■ Type of injury
■ Date and time of treatment
■ Date and time of death
■ A description of distinguishing physical characteristics

Other information related to the individual's DNA, dental records, body fluid, or tissue typing, samples, or analysis cannot be disclosed under this provision.

PHI can also be provided to law enforcement agencies when they are seeking information:

- About a suspected perpetrator of a crime when the report is made by the victim, who is a member of the hospital's workforce.
- To identify or apprehend an individual who has admitted participation in a violent crime that the hospital believes may have caused serious physical harm to a victim, provided that the admission was not made in the course of or based on the individual's request for therapy, counseling, or treatment related to the propensity to commit this type of violent act.
- In response to a request for PHI about a victim of a crime, and the victim agrees. If, because of an emergency or the person's incapacity, the individual cannot agree, the hospital may disclose the PHI if law enforcement officials represent that the PHI is not intended to be used against the victim.
- To prevent or lessen a serious and imminent threat to the health or safety of an individual or the public or to identify or apprehend an individual who appears to have escaped from lawful custody.

In regard to child abuse, neglect, or domestic violence, the PHI can be released when the following applies:

- The reporting of child abuse, adult abuse, neglect, or domestic violence, when authorized by law to receive such reports and based on the exercise of professional judgment, is necessary to prevent serious harm to the individual or others, or in certain other emergency situations. The agreement of the individual is not required.
- Law enforcement is required to be notified, as outlined in local or state law, to report incidents of gunshot or stab wounds or other violent injuries.
- Law enforcement should be alerted to the death of an individual when there is a suspicion that the death resulted from criminal conduct. Information about a decedent may also be shared with medical examiners or coroners to assist them in identifying the decedent, determining the cause of death, or carrying out their other authorized duties.
- PHI should be reported if the covered entity in good faith believes it to be evidence of a crime that occurred on the covered entity's premises.[3]

Occupational Health and Safety Administration

The Occupational Safety and Health Act of 1970 (OSH Act) mandates that all employers have a duty to provide their employees with a workplace free of hazards likely to cause death or serious physical harm. Enforcement of a hazard-free workplace is outlined in Section 5(a)(1) of the OSH Act, called the "General Duty Clause." Until 2015, the General Duty Clause was used by Occupational Health and Safety Administration (OSHA) to enforce their workplace violence guidelines. In January 1989, OSHA published voluntary safety and health guidelines for all employers in the healthcare field that included workplace violence prevention. OSHA's healthcare violence prevention guidelines for reducing workplace violence were developed following a careful review of workplace violence studies, public and private violence prevention programs, and input from stakeholders. The program recommends that employers establish a violence prevention program by tracking and reporting all work-related violence in an effort to monitor and reduce its levels.

In 1989 and today, assaults represent a high percentage of the safety and health hazards reported to OSHA from the healthcare industry. The Bureau of Labor Statistics (BLS) reports that there were 69 homicides in the health services from 1996 to 2000. Although the vast majority of workplace violence consists of nonfatal assaults, the BLS data shows that in 2000, 48% of all nonfatal injuries from occupational assaults and violent acts occurred in healthcare and social services. Most of these occurred in hospitals, nursing and personal care facilities, and residential care services, with nurses, aides, orderlies, and attendants suffering the most nonfatal assaults. Injury rates also show that healthcare and social service workers are at a high risk of violent assault at work. The Department of Justice's (DOJ) National Crime Victimization Survey for 1993–1999 lists average annual rates of nonfatal violent crime by occupation. The average annual rate for nonfatal violent crime for all occupations is 12.6 per 1,000 workers. The average annual rate for physicians is 16.2; for nurses, 21.9; for mental health professionals, 68.2; and for mental health custodial workers, 69. As significant as these numbers are, the actual number is most likely a lot higher. Incidents of violence in the healthcare field generally go underreported because of the perception within the healthcare industry that assaults are part of the job.

Because of the high number of assaults documented by the federal government, in 2004 OSHA published document 3148, "Guidelines for Preventing Workplace Violence for Health Care and Social Service

Workers." This document outlines violence prevention guidelines, identifies common risk factors, and provides feasible solutions to reduce workplace violence in the healthcare setting. The guidelines document was published to help employers eliminate or reduce worker exposure to violence leading to death or injury. The guidelines are designed to assist healthcare employees who work in psychiatric facilities, hospital emergency departments, community mental health clinics, drug abuse treatment clinics, pharmacies, community care facilities, and long-term care facilities. This includes ancillary personnel such as maintenance, dietary, clerical, and security staff.

The guidelines document contains a survey that should be utilized by security as part of its assessment of risk. Areas that have the potential for violence as identified by the document should be surveyed first, followed by any other areas that the healthcare facility has deemed high risk for violence. Recommendations on physical security measures, policies, and procedures that are developed as a result of the survey should be implemented by the hospital so that violent interactions with patients and visitors can be reduced.

In 2012, OHSA published Directive CPL 02-01-052, which went into effective on September 8, 2011. This directive established general policy guidelines and procedures for OSHA field offices to apply when conducting inspections in response to incidents of workplace violence. The directive highlights the steps to be taken in reviewing incidents of workplace violence when considering initiating an inspection. The directive provides guidance on how an OSHA workplace violence case is developed and what steps should be taken to assist employers in reducing workplace violence. This is the first directive by OSHA on enforcement procedures for investigations and inspections resulting from workplace violence incidents in the health-care industry.

In April 2015, the workplace guidelines became regulation. This means that every healthcare organization identified under the OSHA standard must now have a workplace violence program in place. Noncompliance will no longer be enforced through the General Duty Clause but through the workplace violence regulations. In April 2015, OSHA Document 3148 was republished in order to provide guidance on the implementation of a work-place violence program so that healthcare institutions can be compliant. In addition, OSHA recently published a web page on their website specific to healthcare workplace violence. The page provides documents that can help in developing a workplace violence reduction program.[4]

National Center for Missing and Exploited Children

The National Center for Missing and Exploited Children (NCMEC) was established in 1984 and is a nonprofit organization that works with law enforcement, families, and healthcare professionals on issues related to missing and sexually exploited children. The NCMEC has created a coordinated, national response and serves as the national clearinghouse for information on exploited children. The center operates under congressional authorization, under 42 U.S. Code (USC) § 5773. Their role under the U.S. Code is to perform specific tasks that include:

1. Operate the official national resource center and information clearinghouse for missing and exploited children
2. Operate a national 24-hour toll-free telephone line for individuals to report information about any missing child
3. Provide state and local governments, along with public and private nonprofit agencies and individuals, information on services available for missing and exploited children and their families
4. Annually provide the number of children reported to NCMEC as missing, the number of children who are reported as victims of nonfamily abductions, the number of children who are victims of parental kidnappings, and the number of children whose recovery was reported to NCMEC
5. Provide technical assistance and training to law enforcement agencies, state and local governments, elements of the criminal justice system, public and private nonprofit agencies, and individuals in the prevention, investigation, prosecution, and treatment of cases involving missing and exploited children
6. Provide aid to families and law enforcement agencies in locating and recovering missing and exploited children nationally
7. Provide analytical support and technical assistance to law enforcement agencies in locating and recovering missing and exploited children and helping to locate and identify abductors
8. Provide forensic technical assistance and consultation to law enforcement and other agencies in the identification of unidentified deceased children
9. Track the incidence of attempted child abductions in order to identify links and patterns

10. Facilitate the deployment of the National Emergency Child Locator Center to assist in reuniting missing children with their families during periods of national disasters
11. Operate a tip line to provide online users and electronic service providers an effective means of reporting Internet-related child sexual exploitation
12. Work with law enforcement, Internet service providers, electronic payment service providers, and others on methods to reduce the distribution on the Internet of images and videos of sexually exploited children
13. Operate a child victim identification program in order to assist the efforts of law enforcement agencies in identifying victims of child pornography and other sexual crimes
14. Develop and disseminate programs and information to the general public, schools, public officials, youth-serving organizations, and nonprofit organizations, directly or through grants or contracts with public agencies and public and private nonprofit organizations, on the prevention of child abduction and sexual exploitation, and Internet safety

The National Center for Missing and Exploited Children started 30 years ago after several tragic cases, including 6-year-old Etan Patz, who vanished from a New York street on his way to school in 1979. Over the next several years, 29 children and young adults were found murdered in Atlanta. Then in 1981, 6-year-old Adam Walsh was abducted from a Florida shopping mall and later found brutally murdered. When Adam first disappeared, his parents, John and Revé Walsh, turned to law enforcement to help find their son. To their disbelief, there was no coordinated effort among law enforcement to search for Adam on a state or national level and no organization to help them in their desperation. In 1981, and in response to their tragedy, the Walshes established the Adam Walsh Outreach Center for Missing Children in Florida to serve as a national resource for other families with missing children. As the national movement grew, Congress enacted the Missing Children's Act in 1982, which enabled the entry of missing child information into the FBI's National Crime Information Center database, known as NCIC. Former President Ronald Reagan officially opened the National Center for Missing and Exploited Children in 1984, and in 1990 the Adam Walsh Outreach Center merged with NCMEC.

NCMEC receives federal funding for certain core services and utilizes private-sector support from corporations, foundations, and individuals. Over the last 29 years, the center has handled more than 3.7 million calls, circulated billions of photos of missing children, and assisted law enforcement in the recovery of more than 183,000 missing children. NCMEC has trained more than 300,000 law enforcement officers, prosecutors, and healthcare professionals. They deploy members of Team Adam, all retired law enforcement professionals, when children are critically missing, to assist in the search and offer free resources. NCMEC has access to public databases and can help with analysis and mapping. They have forensic artists that can create age-progressed photos and facial and skull reconstructions. They have provided aid that helped U.S. marshals track more than 100,000 noncompliant sex offenders. NCMEC has a team of social services professionals that provide emotional support to families and victims, outreach teams that work in communities to make child safety a daily concern, and education experts who develop free programming.

Regarding infant and child abduction within hospitals, the center publishes three documents specifically for the healthcare environment. These documents offer information on infant abduction specifically within the hospital environment and provide resources to hospital administrators on ways to reduce the probability of abduction. The center also has educational information for parents in order to keep their infants and children safe in the hospital and at home immediately following the birth of their children and subsequent healthcare visits.[5]

Nuclear Regulatory Commission

The U.S. Nuclear Regulatory Commission (NRC) and agreement states regulate the use of radioactive material in order to protect people and the environment. Material licensees have the primary responsibility to maintain the security and accountability of radioactive material in their possession. The events of 9/11 put new emphasis on security to prevent the malicious use of radioactive material, such as a dirty bomb. As a result, the NRC worked with federal and state partners, as well as the international community, to provide appropriate safety and security requirements for radioactive materials without discouraging their beneficial use. Radioactive by-product material provides critical capabilities in the oil and gas, electrical power, construction, and food industries and, most importantly, is used to treat millions of patients each year in diagnostic and therapeutic medical procedures and is used in technology research and development.

Under legislation in Title VI—Nuclear Matters, Subtitle D—Nuclear Security of the Energy Policy Act of 2005, the NRC developed a domestic safeguards program to ensure that special nuclear material within the United States is not stolen or otherwise diverted from civilian facilities for use in terrorist attacks. The program applies safeguards that protect against sabotage, theft, and diversion. This includes material control and accounting for special nuclear materials, along with the physical protection of facilities and/or special nuclear material both at fixed sites and during transportation.

In order to determine how much physical protection is enough, the NRC has a threat assessment program to maintain awareness of the capabilities of potential adversaries and threats to facilities, material, and activities. The National Nuclear Security Administration established the Global Threat Reduction Initiative (GTRI) to identify, secure, remove, and/or facilitate the disposition of high-risk vulnerable nuclear and radiological materials around the world that pose a threat to the United States and the international community. The GTRI works to reduce and protect vulnerable nuclear and radiological material located at civilian sites around the world.

Global Threat Reduction Initiative

Global Threat Reduction Initiative security enhancements focus on increasing detection of unauthorized access and delaying the time it takes an adversary to carry out their task. GTRI provides alarm response training for security and other response personnel. In-device delay (IDD) by installing physical security systems that delay and report any attempts to steal nuclear material located in medical diagnosis, imaging and treatment systems within the hospital. GTRI provides tabletop exercise materials so that hospitals can train in their response to terrorist attacks of their nuclear and radioactive materials. Lastly, GTRI provides off-site source recovery for radioactive sources that are no longer wanted by hospitals and must be removed.[6]

Regulatory Inspection Preparation

As a matter of course, many hospitals' security executives rush to prepare for regulatory surveys from a number of different agencies. Oftentimes the process embraces policy/procedure compliance verification, the auditing of employment records, and verification of training records. Recently, this pressure-packed process has become even more challenging because the Joint Commission, as well as the CMS and other regulatory agencies, no longer gives notice before arriving. This has created changes for many hospitals because these institutions are now required to be compliant-ready 24 hours a day, 7 days a week, as opposed to only once every few years.

To meet this requirement, many hospitals have adapted a 24/7 always-ready approach to managing regulatory audits, ensuring that staff is always prepared for a survey event. Creating an organization that is always ready for an audit takes planning, commitment, and dramatic changes within the organization's culture. Implementation of 24/7 readiness forces hospitals to operate more efficiently and respond to emergencies more effectively and all around reduces the financial burden associated with scrambling to ensure compliance once every three years or so. Implementation of a 24/7 readiness program makes certain that security will consistently meet regulatory compliance.

One of the basic tenets in converting to the 24/7 model is the availability of documents. Policies and procedures, training information, personnel files, and security management plans need to be readily available in the event of a regulatory audit. This means that if the department head is out sick or on vacation, there are other staff available to represent and provide documents that may be requested by a surveyor. It is central to the success of an audit that all documents are accessible at all times and stored in a central location. Documents should be kept in locked facilities that are secure from outside availability but offer easy accessibility at all times. In addition to availability and security, documents should be well organized, properly labeled, and placed in three-ring binders for easy reference. These binders should contain documents that are no more than a year old. Older documents should be stored in a different location.

Maintaining training records helps in readiness and compliance. All training records need to be up-to-date so that auditors can at a glance determine the level of training completed within the compliance period. Training records should include the training outline and learning objectives, the sign-in sheets, and all competencies utilized in the training process.

Additionally, personnel information may be requested by a regulatory auditor, and these records must be available for review. If security personnel are licensed, license records need to be available. The security department needs to track license expiration dates and recertification dates to ensure that licenses present in the employment file are current. The security department must also ensure that all licensed staff have primary-source proof of licensure maintained within their employment file.

The most important documents that a regulator will review are department policies and procedures. As a rule of thumb, policies should be updated every two to three years. Typically, policy review is limited to only a quick scan of the policy, seeking out misspelled words or changes in titles, addresses, or phone numbers. A complete audit should be conducted periodically on all policies and procedures to ensure that implementation actually mimics written policy. In order to achieve 24/7 readiness, policies should be tested every two to three years by selecting a small number each year to critique and ensure compliance. The compliance process should include a review of the written documents to help catch spelling and grammar errors, as well as scheduling meetings with all involved parties via a tabletop exercise or mapping to review the procedural operations, ensuring they are compliant to what is written in the policy.

Processes should be developed and implemented that allow for the regular auditing of equipment to ensure proper operation. For example, the National Center for Missing and Exploited Children recommends weekly checks of the infant banding system to make certain that it is operating properly. All security equipment should be inspected on a regularly scheduled basis to ensure optimum functionality. As a matter of practice, items from flashlights to card readers to camera recorders need to be inspected. Equipment compliance requires that management institute an inspection schedule that is spread out over a finite period of time listing specific mandates on which pieces of equipment are to be checked, when they are to be checked, and how they are to be checked. For example, all of the cameras in Building A are checked in January, the cameras in Building B are checked in February, etc. Equipment checks can encompass 100% of the total or a percentage of the total number of devices in place. If it is decided to check a percentage of the total number of devices, then these same devices should not be tested again until 100% of the devices are checked. An example of a detailed inspection of an infant abduction system would be to test every, or a percentage of every, transmitter, portal, and ceiling receiver to ensure proper activation. Portal checks would include the locking of doors and the activation of alarms at all portals.

Training is critical to the readiness process. It is paramount that all staff working on all shifts is knowledgeable in every single policy and procedure that relates to security. In order for that to become a reality, training must be a continuous ongoing exercise. Training must occur on an annual basis at a minimum, with a midyear test or competency check. In addition, when procedures change immediate action must occur in order to ensure that staff is apprised of the change and modifications.

One method that ensures training compliance is the use of competencies. Competencies are tests that highlight the key components of the training program and are used by educators to improve retention levels. Competencies can be written tests, observations, drills, or any combination of the three. It is important to remember that training alone may not be enough; procedures may have to be implemented that support the initial training and reinforce the key learning objectives between training sessions. The best method of accomplishing this is either via observation testing and review or through drill and exercise critiquing. Both methods allow for hands-on review and educational reinforcement of the initial training framework.

The key to the successful implementation of a readiness program is the development of monitoring processes that will ensure that the program complies all of the time. The use of departmental standards and metrics to monitor and measure compliance works best for the implementation of a monitoring program. Department standards are developed to set a minimal level of readiness, and metrics are implemented to measure the compliance.[7]

References

1. The Joint Commission. www.jointcommission.org.
2. Center for Medicare and Medicaid Services. *Regulations and Guidance*. https://www.cms.gov/Regulations-and-Guidance/Regulations-and-Guidance.html.
3. U.S. Department of Health and Human Resources. *OCR Privacy Brief, Summary of the HIPAA Privacy Rule*. 2003.
4. Occupational Safety and Health Administration. *Workplace Violence*. https://www.osha.gov/SLTC/workplaceviolence/.
5. National Center for Missing and Exploited Children. *About Us*. http://www.missingkids.com/footer/about.
6. Nuclear Regulatory Commission Office of Federal and State Materials and Environmental Management Programs. *The Global Threat Reduction Initiative (GTRI), Domestic Threat Reduction Program & Federally Funded Voluntary Security Enhancements for High-Risk Radiological Materials*. NRC Regulatory Issue Summary 2008-23. October 3, 2008. https://www.nrc.gov/docs/ML1031/ML103190127.pdf.
7. Luizzo, Anthony and Bernard J. Scaglione. Aspects of preparing for a regulatory audit. *Journal of Healthcare Protection Management*, Vol. 26, No. 1, pp.14–20, 2010.

Chapter 2

Management of Personnel

Introduction

The management of security personnel differs from the management of personnel in other industries. Generally, security officers are spread far apart and often work in isolated areas. Because security officers are typically spread distances apart, support and response can be minutes or even hours away. In the security field, security officers have to make their own decisions. Healthcare security is no different. Because of the physical layout of healthcare institutions and the distance of clinics and doctor's offices, the security officer must make individual decisions. The management of healthcare security officers requires a specific management style that allows for a large span of control and supports individual decision making.

Span of Control

The typical industry standard staff-to-supervisor ratio is about ten workers to one supervisor. In most industries, ten employees to one supervisor works well because workers are stationed close together in work cubicles or offices and are generally located in close proximity to their supervisor. When staff are spread out over a few thousand or million square feet, the supervision ratio of ten to one is not effective. In the security field, the staff-to-supervisor ratio should be lower. Generally, a ratio of seven or eight officers to one supervisor works best. When officers are spread great distances apart, like in healthcare, where off-site clinics or offices can be miles apart, the ratio of four or five officers to one supervisor works best, depending on the work environment.

Theories relating to span of control go back as far as 1933. V. A. Graicunas used assumptions on mental capacity and attention span to develop a set of management-to-subordinate relationships. He distinguished three types of interactions: direct single relationships, cross-relationships, and direct group relationships. Direct single relationships are the number of workers reporting to a supervisor. Cross-relationships are the relationships between these workers, and direct group relationships are the relationship the supervisor has to his workers as a group. Based on worker tasks, each interaction type is considered within the total number of interactions within the organization. Span of control is determined on the number of total interactions between a supervisor and their subordinates. Henry Fayol was a French mining engineer who developed a general theory of business administration that is often called "Fayolism." In 1916, he published his experiences in the book *Administration Industrielle et Générale.* Fayol's work became more generally known with the 1949 publication of the general and industrial administration article "Administration industrielle et générale." Fayol's span of control theory was based on the geographical dispersion of workers and the continued need for face-to-face meetings in the management of those workers. In 1988, Elliott Jaques determined that a manager can have as many subordinates as he can know personally, so that he can assess the effectiveness of employees based on their personal relationship.

The theories presented by V. A. Graicunas, Henry Fayol, and Elliott Jaques help in the determination of span of control. These factors include geographical dispersion, the capability of employees, the capability of the supervisor, and the similarity of employee tasks. Geographical dispersion refers to how widely employees are dispersed throughout the organization.[1] In healthcare, officers are spread over great distances, which requires a lower span of control ratio, again generally four or five officers to one supervisor. The capability of workers means their ability to do the job. Employees who need little supervision, like Theory Y employees, need a lower span of control. The supervisor's experience, knowledge of the job, relationship to his or her employees, and time available to supervise determines the span of control as well. A highly experienced and knowledgeable supervisor can control a larger group of employees. Highly trained and developed employees need less supervision, so the span of control can be greater. Additionally, if worker tasks are similar, then the span of control can be greater as well.

Management of Personnel

The management of personnel is a complicated and challenging process, especially when staff are placed distances apart and many times have to make decisions on their own. The management style that is necessary to supervise security personnel must allow for this type of environment. Most authors that write in the field of security reference Douglas McGregor's workforce motivational theory, "Theory X, Theory Y," as the best model to supervise security personnel. These two contrasting ideas explain the general behavior of workers and how these two management styles can be effective in supervising staff. Theory X, Theory Y was an idea devised by Douglas McGregor in his 1960 book *The Human Side of Enterprise*. It established a fundamental distinction between management styles. McGregor first outlined his ideas in a speech at MIT's Sloan School of Management in April 1957. Close to Abraham Maslow, and influenced by him, McGregor became a significant counter to the thinking and influence of scientific management.[2] His central idea was that there are two fundamentally different styles of management. One of them he called Theory X, and the other Theory Y. Theory X assumes that individuals are reluctant to work and require strict supervision, external rewards, and penalties. Theory X reflects an underlying belief that there is an inherent human tendency to avoid work. This theory assumes that individuals are work-shy and constantly in need of supervision. In contrast, Theory Y assumes that people inherently love to work and are committed to working. They are motivated, have high job satisfaction, and work without direct supervision. Theory Y assumes that individuals go to work of their own accord, because work is the only way in which they have a chance of satisfying their (high-level) need for achievement and self-respect. Theories X and Y are not seen as opposite ends of the same continuum, but two different continua in themselves.

Theory X

Theory X is a pessimistic view of the average worker. This theory assumes that the average worker has little or no motivation to work, shying away from work and responsibilities. Theory X managers believe that their employees are less intelligent, lazy, and work solely for a sustainable income. Because of this assumption, Theory X concludes that the average worker is more productive when a "hands-on" approach to management is utilized. This theory believes that all work should be closely monitored and given a direct reward or reprimand according to the worker's outcomes. This managerial style is most effective when used to motivate a workforce that is unmotivated to perform. According to Douglas McGregor, there are two approaches to managing Theory X employees, the "hard" approach and the "soft" approach. The hard approach utilizes close supervision, intimidation, and imminent punishment to supervise workers. However, when implemented, this approach can create a hostile, minimally cooperative workforce that resentments management. The soft approach is the literal opposite, characterized by leniency and less strict application of the rules in hopes for high moral and cooperative employees. However, the soft approach can result in an entitled, low-output workforce. McGregor believes that somewhere between these two approaches is the best management style for Theory X employees.

Overall, Theory X is the most effective management style in terms of consistency of work. When managers and supervisors are in complete control of the work, there is a more systematic and uniform product or workflow. Theory X employees work best in a routine or mundane work environment, like security work. Utilizing Theory X in security work allows management to motivate employees and keep them on track toward their assigned job functions and goals.

Theory Y

In contrast, Theory Y assumes that people in the workforce are internally motivated, enjoy working, and work to better themselves without a direct reward in return. Theory Y states that workers thrive on the challenges that they may face in the workplace and like to improve their personal performance. Workers tend to take full responsibility for their work and do not require or need constant supervision in order to create a quality and high-standard product. Theory Y managers relate to workers on a more personal and relatable level, as opposed to a more conductive and discipline-based relationship. While Theory Y may seem like the best option, it does have some disadvantages. While there is a more personal and individualistic feel, there is no consistency and uniformity in the workflow. The lax enforcement of rules and practices can result in an inconsistent product, which can be disastrous to quality standards.[3]

Douglas McGregor's theories have their positive and negative sides but relate to the management of the real world very well when considering the positive sides to each theory. In summary, Theory X people need more supervision and recognition, whereas Theory Y people need little supervision but continued reinforcement of the rules. When you look closely at the two theories and think about the people you supervise, most persons do fit into either one of the two theories.

Managing Personnel Using Theory X and Theory Y

McGregor's Theory X, Theory Y is known as a contingency theory. A contingency theory is an organizational or management theory that claims that there is no one way or theory to best manage people. Instead, the contingency theory believes that the best management practice is dependent on the people and the type of work performed. A contingent leader effectively applies different management styles of leadership in different situations. The contingency model works within the management of subordinates and supervisors in the security field because of the spacing of personnel and the tasks associated with security work. Using several management practices to supervise staff promotes a content workforce. Douglas McGregor's theories work well as a contingency model for the management of security personnel. The utilization of Theory X, Theory Y management effectively motivates workers while allowing them to meet their hierarchal needs. By applying both principles in the management of officers, the administration of personnel is easier and will be more successful. Staff that seem unmotivated or require constant supervision are Theory X employees. Supervising these staff requires close supervision, constant reward, and continued reinforcement of their job functions. When these basic needs are provided to Theory X employees, they will be successful and happy at work and flourish. In contrast, Theory Y employees need to be left alone; they do not want to be closely supervised and are motivated by making their own decisions. These employees may not want to learn the specifics of the job, but periodic refreshment of the job functions will help them stay on track. However, training for Theory Y workers needs to be conducted in a formal educational setting and not presented in a way that is perceived as controlling, demanding, or a requirement.[3]

The use of these two theories requires the categorization of all staff into one of the two. Sitting down and analyzing staff performance and their need for supervision can assist in the identification of each employee's classification. For example, if an officer is the type that constantly calls for a supervisor or will not make decisions on their own, they are a Theory X employee. Unsupervised, they are the staff that drifts off post or is constantly conversing with other officers or staff while on post. If they are the last ones out of the locker room at the start of their shift and the last one on post, they are Theory X employees. In contrast, if they are the first officers out of the locker room, then they are Theory Y employees. If they complain when a supervisor stops at their post too often, then they are a Theory Y employee. If they make decisions while on post and occasionally make decisions that are not exactly in compliance with policy and procedure, then they are a Theory Y employee.

When managing Theory X and Theory Y workers, supervisors and managers need to remember that each officer, depending on their classification, is supervised differently. The Theory X employees should be the first officers visited after the shift has started to ensure that they are on post and doing their job, and the last officers to be visited right before shift change. Frequent post inspections for these individuals will be necessary during the tour. Post checks should be about ensuring that officers are on post, standing in the right location, following post procedures, and not spending time unnecessarily socializing with everyone. Supervisor interactions with these officers should always be professional and should continually reinforce the behaviors that management is looking for. Interactions with Theory X workers should never be punitive, negative, critical, or demeaning. However, negative reinforcement works when necessary for Theory X employees who do not continually comply with the rules or who continually make poor decisions. Theory X workers require constant praise and positive reinforcement. Verbal praise works, but more meaningful recognition provides for a more engaged employee. Verbal acknowledgment should be frequent and consistent. Awards and gifts for a job well done are always appreciated by a Theory X worker.

Theory Y officers do not require constant supervision; they can make their own decisions and feel comfortable doing so. However, Theory Y workers tend to make decisions that can sometimes be contrary to policy. A continual review of their post assignment in detail will help keep them on track. For example, if officers are told not to leave their post but an officer assists a handicapped patient into the hospital and leaves their post to do so, they are a Theory Y officer, making a good decision that is not necessarily within policy. The supervision of Theory Y officers is the continued reinforcement of rules in a positive way, like roll call review, annual training, and occasional post inspections. These officers do not need constant praise or job reinforcement but do require a path for continued responsibility and promotion. Theory Y workers are your source for internal promotion opportunities. Continued praise, negative reinforcement, and punishment do not work for Theory Y workers and should be avoided.

Supervisors are an important part of the management of security personnel. Supervisors can be either Theory X or Theory Y personnel themselves and need to be supervised accordingly. There should be close management of Theory X supervisors or managers and less management of Theory Y supervisors and managers. Like the supervision of the officers, Theory X supervisors or managers need constant checking to ensure that they are doing their job. Continual reinforcement of their duties and praise are necessary to manage Theory X supervisors. Again, negative reinforcement works with Theory X employees and can work with supervisors as well. Theory X supervisors work well in a structured environment run by the enforcement of strict rules and procedures. The disadvantage to Theory X supervisors or managers is that they are not comfortable with making independent decisions. They rely on others to make decisions for them. The Theory Y supervisor or manager is self-reliant. They work on their own and feel comfortable making their own decisions. Theory Y supervisors and managers need rule reinforcement on a constant basis. Again, if reinforcement is seen like micromanagement, they will become unmotivated and ineffective. Theory Y supervisors and managers have one disadvantage: their independent decision making does not always work in a rule and discipline–oriented culture. Although they will do a great job motivating workers with little or no supervision, they create a department that is not consistent in the enforcement of the rules, and because of this style, at times, they may be seen as showing favoritism toward certain officers.

When it comes to the application of Theory X, Theory Y, consider combining like types of employees and supervisors when possible. The easiest way to supervise and motivate personnel is to have them manage by their same style of person—Theory X being supervised by Theory X and Theory Y being supervised by Theory Y. Supervising like management types makes the job easier and provides an environment where officers, supervisors, and managers can be more successful. Because of the increasingly complex role of the security director in today's healthcare environment, managing multiple types of supervisors or managers makes the management of the department more challenging. When hiring supervisors and managers, make sure that they fit the particular management style of the persons they are supervising or provide them with the education and skill set to supervise their opposite type successfully. Patience and a thorough understanding of each management type and how it is applied to each worker will make the security department operate more effectively and will help to provide engaged, motivated employees.

Staff Supervision and Engagement

Staff engagement is an extremely important part of the security program. When engaged, employees provide a professional work environment and a higher level of security for hospital occupants. Engagement is all about the security department culture. This has to occur from the security director position down. The security director must be committed to establishing a culture of engagement for the security department and work with administrative staff to encourage and promote that culture. Creating an environment where staff are engaged involves several factors. First, staff have to be managed correctly, utilizing Theory X or Theory Y. They need to be motivated to do their jobs. They need to be properly trained and understand their job in detail, as well as their function within the hospital organization. They need to have the opportunity to expand their role, be promoted and/or recognized for their work, and have a set work schedule so that they can manage their personal life. Putting these things all together encourages an employee that is motivated and engaged.

Theory X, Theory Y motivates staff by managing them in the way that best fits each employee's particular needs. As mentioned earlier, each employee has a specific set of needs that are necessary to be met in order for them to be motivated and engaged at work. Some employees require constant and close supervision, Theory X workers. That means their supervisor must keep a close eye on them to ensure that they are doing the job correctly. When found to be doing the job correctly, Theory X employees have to be recognized and rewarded for their accomplishments. In contrast, Theory Y employees do not need or want direct or close supervision. What motivates them is the freedom to do their job without constant monitoring by management. Theory Y employees want to be free to do the job the way they see fit. This can make the implementation of the security program difficult because Theory Y employees like to do it their own way. To be successful and motivate Theory Y personnel, continued reinforcement of their job functions is needed—not enough to make them feel micromanaged, but enough for them to stay within the application of their job, not changing policy and procedure.

Scheduling Staff

Many times, both the employee and the employer forget that employment is a contractual relationship where the employer controls job functions and schedule, and the employee carries out the job functions and works the hours designated by the employer. In exchange for carrying out the employer's work function and work hours, the employee gets compensated. However, many times this contractual relationship becomes blurry; the employer needs more or different work hours or the employee's life changes and they need different work hours. The conflict between the two often-times results in bad blood for both parties and good employees either leave or become unmotivated. All organizations need to have staff coverage that works best for the organization and to do so at the least possible cost. As part of the worker–employer contract, the employer has the right to adjust and modify an employee's work schedule to fit the needs of the organization. This is especially true in healthcare security where operations extend 24 hours a day, 7 days a week, 365 days a year. However, security directors need to work hard to provide a work schedule that fits both the organization's and the employee's needs.

The most overlooked motivator in the engagement of staff is the work schedule. Security staff, along with all other employees in the workforce, have personal lives and the desire to be social outside of the work environment. One of Maslow's basic needs is social interaction. So, it is very important to provide each employee with a work schedule that allows for social interaction outside of the work environment. Officers, supervisors, and all other security department staff should have a set work schedule. Consistency of a work schedule allows employees the opportunity for a social life. Everyone knows that there are times when employees must stay and cover a shift, but in general staff should have a fixed work schedule. Their shift and days off should be consistent. Days off should be together when possible and their work schedule should not change unless at the employee's request or an emergent situation within the hospital. Scheduling of staff can include the rotation of weekends off. Staff should have every other, every third, or every fourth weekend off. This again will allow staff to have a more stable work environment. When the hospital has to change a work schedule, both the employer and employee should be given as much notice as possible before the change takes effect, allowing both parties the opportunity to adjust to the change.

A standard shift schedule looks like the one shown in Figure 2.1, allowing for two days off in a row or every other weekend off.

A standard schedule provides officers with two days off in a row and consistent coverage for the hospital seven days a week. If less staff is needed on the weekend, then more officers can have Saturday and Sunday off or use the schedule shown in Figure 2.2, with every other weekend off.

Hospital Security Department Work Schedule

Officer Name	Sunday	Monday	Tuesday	Wednesday	Thursday	Friday	Saturday	Sunday	Monday	Tuesday	Wednesday	Thursday	Friday	Saturday
Officer 1	■	■									■	■		
Officer 2	■	■									■	■		
Officer 3		■	■									■	■	
Officer 4		■	■									■	■	
Officer 5			■	■									■	■
Officer 6			■	■									■	■
Officer 7				■	■			■						■
Officer 8				■	■			■						■
Officer 9					■	■		■	■					
Officer 10					■	■		■	■					
Officer 11						■	■		■	■				
Officer 12						■	■		■	■				
Officer 13	■						■			■	■			
Officer 14	■						■			■	■			
Total on Duty	10	10	10	10	10	10	10	10	10	10	10	10	10	10

*Black Box Signifies Day Off

Figure 2.1   Standard work schedule—two days off in a row.

Hospital Security Department Work Schedule

Officer Name	Sunday	Monday	Tuesday	Wednesday	Thursday	Friday	Saturday	Sunday	Monday	Tuesday	Wednesday	Thursday	Friday	Saturday
Officer 1														
Officer 2														
Officer 3														
Officer 4														
Officer 5														
Officer 6														
Officer 7														
Officer 8														
Officer 9														
Officer 10														
Officer 11														
Officer 12														
Officer 13														
Officer 14														
Total on Duty	7	11	11	12	12	12	7	7	12	11	11	11	12	7

*Black Box Signifies Day Off

Figure 2.2 Every other weekend work schedule.

This schedule provides officers with the opportunity to have two weekends off a month. The downside to this schedule is that officers may need a weekend day off for a wedding or family function. Usually in this case, officers are asked to switch weekends with other officers, making the schedule potentially very complicated. In addition, as you can see, this schedule dramatically limits the number of officers that work the weekend, requiring more staff or part-time staff to work on the weekends.

Staff Performance

How management cares for its employees is key to the engagement process. Rarely is management trained in the praise and discipline process so that employees remain motivated and engaged. Most important to motivation and employee satisfaction is how management handles the performance aspects of the individual employee—how the employee is disciplined and praised and how their performance is documented. Many times, the performance appraisal process is not correctly tied in to how an employee performs their job. Performance appraisals are seen by many managers as punishment utilized as feedback on how poor an employee is performing. Negative behavior is the only behavior discussed and documented during work and when annual performance appraisals are conducted. Many managers do not understand or have not been properly trained in performance feedback and performance evaluations.

The process of performance evaluation starts on the day of employment. Every employee has a probationary period that they must complete in order to become a permanent part of the security team. Again, as part of the contract between the employee and the employer, a period is allotted so that the employer can evaluate the employee, and often forgotten, the employee evaluates the employer. During this period, it is important that the employee learn the job functions, their work schedule, and exactly what is expected of them as an employee of the hospital security department. That is why orientation training is so very important and should extend well into the probationary period. For example, if the probationary period is six months, then training should be at least four months. During that time, the new employee should complete all of their training and orientation requirements. There should be continued feedback between management and the employee— ensuring that the employee understands the job and its requirements and expectations, and again, mostly forgotten, that the employer meets the needs of the employee. During this time, there should be regular documented meetings with the employee to ensure that he or she understands all aspects of the job. These meetings should have a standardized agenda used for all new employees and meetings should be documented for the employment record. These meetings should review department expectations and the employee's roles within the department and organization, and continually reinforce job functions. In addition, these meetings should allow for frank dialogue on job performance and encourage questions from the employee. They should allow the employee to freely ask questions to clarify issues and help them understand their role within the security department.

After an employee has passed probation and is now part of the security team, performance review needs to continue. Every employee should have the opportunity to sit one-on-one with their supervisor in order to hear feedback on their performance and express their needs as part of the employment process. Regularly scheduled meetings with the employee should continue after probation ends. These meetings do not have to be as frequent but should proactively address positive and negative behavior as well as allow for the employee to provide feedback on their work environment. For example, if an officer is getting close to violating the sick time policy, their supervisor should sit down with the employee and review the sick policy. During the meeting the employee should be asked if assistance is needed to help correct the problem. Regular meetings are also a perfect time to provide additional training and information about the job, hospital, and other departments so that the employee gets continual reinforcement of job requirements. These meetings should have a standardized agenda so that all employees are treated the same and supervisors are consistent in the management of staff. These sessions should be documented as well. If supervisors continually meet with staff on a regular basis to provide both positive and negative feedback, annual evaluations are easy to complete and execute since all the information included in the evaluation has already been documented and presented to the employee throughout the year. Annual evaluations should not be a time for employees to hear new things about their performance. This practice does not motivate employees and can create poor performance. No one wants to hear about new negative behavior that occurred months earlier when memories have faded.

Recruiting the Right Staff

Staff recruitment can be an arduous task. The process can be difficult when not implemented properly. Again, many directors or recruiters forget what the recruitment process is all about. The purpose of the hiring process is to successfully recruit the people that best fit into the organization and are motivated to perform the job. It's about the employer and the potential employee evaluating a position in the hospital to see if it works best for them; it's a two-way street. For the security department, the process should be designed to hire staff that are motivated to perform the tasks that are outlined in the job description. For the potential employee, the job needs to fit their personal needs (Maslow's needs), lifestyle, and benefit requirements.

Before the hiring process can take place, there is some prerecruitment homework that needs to be completed. First, the security department needs to formulate the type of person that best fits within their organization. Much of this information can be provided from the training program. Are they a Theory X or Theory Y person? Do they understand the basic requirements of the job? Are they a good fit for the security team and the overall organization? The best way to determine what type of person fits within the security organization is to ask successful people who are already working in the security department. They are the best indicator of how well a new employee will work with the team and be motivated in the job. The personality, background, and experience of your best employees are clear indicators of successful recruitment of new employees. In addition to the personality and experience, basic skills needed to be evaluated. Skills are determined as part of the training curriculum development and should be used to set the requirements for a potential new hire.

The candidate interview process is the tool that helps in the determination for selecting future employees. Although very limited in its ability to assess an individual to see if they are the right fit for the organization, when conducted correctly it can help in the determination of an appropriate candidate. The interview process allows the employer and the employee to evaluate each other in order to determine if the job is a best fit for both parties. As mentioned previously, this is often overlooked, and when not addressed it leads to the hiring of an employee who is not a fit for the organization.

The interview process should start with a formal question and answer session. This includes a set of standard questions that are used for each candidate in each job classification. These questions should be behavioral and skill based. Questions should be approved by the human resource department and include actual job situations and job skills. Questions should be phased to obtain answers that will test behaviors that are required for the job, like communication, patience, and customer service, and uncover negative behaviors like anger, excessive use of physical force, rudeness, or acting out of the scope of the job. Behavioral questions include:

- Could you describe a difficult problem and how you dealt with it?
- What were some of the things you did not like about your last job?
- What do you consider your most significant weaknesses?
- How do you accept criticism?
- What is the most difficult situation you have faced?
- What are some of the things that bother you?
- Do you prefer working with others or alone?
- How do you get along with different types of people?
- Can you give me an example of a project that didn't work out well?
- What are some of the things you and your supervisor have disagreed on?

Skill-based questions should be included as well, questions that allow candidates to describe how they would solve an issue or deal with specific problems or situations. Skill or competency-based questions are more systematic then behavioral-based questions, targeting a specific skill or competency. Skill-based interview questions include:

- Give me an example of how you would explain a complicated procedure to someone who was new to the situation.
- Describe a work-related problem you had to face recently. What procedures did you use to deal with it?
- Describe your normal methods of assigning work to subordinates.
- Give me an example of a time you found it necessary to make an exception to the rules in order to get something done.
- Tell me about the best boss you ever had. What made him or her so great to work for?
- What did you do to help your subordinates set performance objectives last year?
- Have you ever had an occasion when you misunderstood someone else's instructions? Why do you think that happened?

Answers to questions should be scored with a standardized scoring system so that interview evaluations are consistent and standardized. A scale evaluating positive and negative answers should be used, and an area for comments should be present and should be completed for every question asked. Every answered question should have a comment written about the candidate's answer. This can help in the final determination of several candidates when scores, experience, and qualifications are similar. Once the interview of the candidate is completed, the process is not done. Make sure that the applicant has the opportunity to ask questions about the job. Once all questioning has been answered, the interviewer should describe the job, duties, work hours, and expectations to the candidate. Then the applicant should be walked around the security department and given a tour of some of the posts and jobs by a supervisor. In addition, the applicant should stand post with an officer for a few minutes in order to have time to speak to a current employee. After that process is complete, the candidate should sit with the interviewer one more time so that the candidate has the opportunity to ask more questions.

Employee Onboarding

Onboarding a new employee should be a very systematic and detailed process. As mentioned earlier in this chapter, the process should take time, up to four months or two-thirds of the probationary period. During that time the officer should be exposed to all posts and job assignments, and have access to staff in order to learn and evaluate the job. Training for new employees should not be conducted all at once. Generally, the orientation process ends within a week or two of the start date and all training is conducted during that time. Training should be conducted over an extended period, not just the first few weeks of employment. The new officer should be exposed to the job as quickly as possible so that the security department can assess the new employee and the new employee can assess their new position. For example, many hospitals require security staff to release bodies from the morgue. Sometimes, new employees become unmotivated or even leave the job when they realize that they have to fulfill that job function, which they are not typically exposed to until after probation or months into the job.

Orientation is an important part of the onboarding process and is the easiest time for an employee termination or an employee leaving if the job is not a good fit. Documentation of the orientation process is so important at this point of the employment process. The security department must be able to fairly and effectively evaluate a new employee and document their ability to do the job. A standard checklist of orientation activities should be developed that incorporates all training and processes, like what posts the employee has held, and provide not only the dates of the events, but also a summary evaluation of each item or event. A more detailed sheet or evaluation should be created and kept for each activity that a new employee completes. A sample of an orientation checklist is contained in Appendix 4.

The Promotion Process

Often, the internal promotional process is overlooked and very few resources are allocated to make the promotional process successful. Repeatedly, employees are promoted to supervisor or manager because of their longevity or because they excel in their current position. Sometimes promotion due to longevity or strong work performance is successful; however, just as frequently this type of promotion is not successful, and the individual fails or stays in a supervisory position but is inefficient. Often, few resources and time are spent on a successful transition or onboarding of promoted personnel or persons hired into a supervisory position. The lack of commitment to training frequently results in ineffective management and unengaged workers.

The promotion or recruitment of management personnel should be based on a standard set of criteria connected to a specific set of skills determined in advance. As discussed above, before the recruitment process starts, a set of skills and job requirements should be determined. Whether an internal promotion or hired from outside of the organization, the interview process should be a formal process and set up the same as described above. For internal candidates, a tour of the facility does not have to occur, but for both internal and external recruits a tour of the supervisor process should occur. Supervisor post checks, paperwork review, and a review of job responsibilities should occur.

Regardless of whether the new hire is an internal or external candidate, the training process should continue for two-thirds of the probationary period. During the first few weeks of probation, the new employee should be exposed to all job functions so that both parties can evaluate the job and performance. The remainder of the probationary period is for education and training. New management should be continually learning so that when probation is over, they are fully prepared to supervise staff. Education and training should include courses on how to be a supervisor, becoming a new supervisor, and what to expect when you become a supervisor. These courses should be given to both promoted and recruited personnel. Even if the new hire came from an institution where they were already in a supervisory position, they should still attend new supervision courses. Formal education should be conducted by a third-party firm, not conducted in-house. Outside, third-party courses allow the new supervisor to learn without the pressure of trying to perform for their new employer. Another important process for the success of a new supervisor or manager is mentoring. Started during the probationary period, every new supervisory person should be given a mentor to help them be successful in the job. Mentors should be from outside of the security department and be at the same supervisory level. Mentoring should continue past the probationary period and extend into the first year of employment. If a mentoring process does not exist within the hospital, the security department should consider creating one. However, security leadership should take courses on mentoring and find a local institution that utilizes mentoring to learn how best to start and run a mentoring program.

References

1. Wikipedia. Span of Control. https://en.wikipedia.org/wiki/Span_of_control.
2. Wikipedia. Theory X and Theory Y. https://en.wikipedia.org/wiki/Theory_X_and_Theory_Y.
3. The Economist. Guru: Douglas McGregor. October 3, 2008. http://www.economist.com/node/12366698.

Chapter 3

Training Security Personnel

Introduction

The training of staff is the single most important component in a highly effective security program. A comprehensive training program creates engaged, motivated employees who have a clear understand of their job and can be effective members of the hospital team. In order to create and sustain a high level of staff performance, training must be extensive and continuous, with focus on the processes and behaviors that management considers most important to the security staff's job, like customer service, communication, leadership, writing, or presentation skills. The proper education of staff needs to be "behavioral" or "functional" based, developed from criteria specific to the organization. The goal of a solid training program provides proficiency in all areas of an employee's job functions. In its conclusion, the training program should equip security staff with the knowledge necessary for them to make competent decisions while in the field and ensure that those decisions are consistent with the hospital's mission and department's policy and procedure. It is paramount that training be part of the everyday operations of the security program. Training should be reinforced on a regular basis to ensure that staff maintain a high level of knowledge and competency. They should be experts at their jobs.

Creating the Training Program Curriculum

A training program that is effective in teaching staff their jobs is implemented with the creation of a training curriculum. Every hospital security department should have a training curriculum that outlines the department training program, detailing the training subjects, methods of teaching, lesson plans, etc. Developing a curriculum sets the tone for the entire security education program, determining the overall results or capabilities attained through the training process. It also serves as a script for instructors, so that training is consistent and targeted. Developing a security department curriculum starts with an assessment of the department training requirements. This assessment helps to develop the training strategy, defines training objectives and goals, determines learning methods, creates training documentation, and develops a program evaluation. The training assessment should include:

- The formation of a training policy that outlines the purpose, scope, and process for the training program.
- The creation of training goals and objectives. Goals and objective should be specific to each training topic and job classification. They should provide a basic outline to the intent, result, and timeline of the training program.
- The creation of a training scope. The scope outlines key skills and job tasks or functions that staff will need to achieve based on the curriculum objectives. The scope is created by reviewing all of the material necessary for the security staff to understand and conduct their jobs in an efficient and effective manner.
- The subjects of study. This determination is made based on regulatory requirements and other subjects that are deemed necessary for all staff to effectively carry out their job.
- Competencies, which are the specific tasks or functions that are necessary in order to complete a process or procedure and demonstrate that staff understand the concepts within the training topic, like when force can be used and how staff should take down or hand cuff a perpetrator.
- The frequency of training. This may be determined by regulatory requirements or internally based on the job assessment.
- An annual review of the training program and its effectiveness. This includes an established system of curriculum evaluation, trainer feedback, and competency compliance levels.

Training Policy

The training program should be outlined in the form of a written policy. The training policy should provide a statement outlining the training program, its purpose, and its philosophy, along with a summary of the training program.

The policy should incorporate all job levels and include a policy statement, purpose, and procedure for the training of all staff. Written within the procedure should be a summary of the training objectives and goals, standards to be met by training of the staff and the training data, and its measurement that will determine the success of the training program. (See the Sample Training Policy in Appendix 5.)

Training Goals and Objectives

Every training program should have a set of goals and objectives that incorporate the hospital's mission, values, and goals. Training goals and objectives should contain the outcomes expected of the curriculum, outline the major content focus areas (as specific as possible), suggest instructional strategies, and include performance objectives and time frames for completion. Training goals and objectives, like all departmental goals, should be reviewed on an annual basis and adjust objectives based on changes in regulation, in hospital goals, or within the security department.

Training Scope

The training scope focuses on the knowledge and skill set that staff will require in order to correctly carry out their job. The job scope is defined as an action or sequence of actions that contributes to the completion of a specific work objective. The scope provides a clear, complete picture of what needs to be done, how it is being done, and why it is being done. Scopes can be written in the format of a statement presenting a standardized, concise description of worker actions. Job scopes need to be completed for all job levels, from the director of security on down. Each job classification should have a written job scope as part of the training curriculum. Developing a job scope means assessing training needs. This process starts with a review of all legal and regulatory requirements. In healthcare security, there are a number of agencies that regulate security officer training. These include the Joint Commission, the Centers for Medicare & Medicaid Services, the Occupational Safety and Health Administration, and state and local security officer licensing legislation (see Chapter 1 for more information). Many states require security staff to be licensed. Licensure may include specific training requirements. Once the regulatory requirements are determined, each job description within the department must be assessed, breaking down each job description into the specific job tasks outlined within the document, for example, good writing skills or knowing how to use a computer or specific software programs. Next, a review should be conducted of all post or job duties/assignments, again, breaking down each job function or duty, for example, having situational awareness when manning a post or writing neatly when filling out a patient valuables form. All reports, like daily activity reports, incident reports, or logs, that the security department utilizes should be review and broken down into the job tasks required in order to complete each form. Written policies and procedures need to be reviewed, determining their specific job functions, for example, taking decisive action when responding to a fire alarm or using listening skills and extracting information when receiving an emergency call. Once completed, this assessment will provide a list of job tasks and functions that are required for each job category. This set of tasks should then be incorporated into the training scope for each job category.

Training Standards

A sound training program should contain standards—specific topics, behaviors, and knowledge that are taught to all staff. Standards provide for the consistent application of training throughout the entire department. Standards give the security department and each staff member a clearer understanding of their role and job expectations. Every training course, lesson plan, etc., should have specific standards that are part of the curriculum—standards such as minimum test score, course completion dates, use of certain information when teaching the course, and handouts or information given to students. Together, designated standards will maintain a consistent level of education and provide staff with the behaviors and information that is most important in performing their job.

The Lesson Plan

In order to teach the training topics specified by your particular training program, a lesson plan for each training session or topic must be developed. Every training subject should have a written lesson plan that outlines how training will be conducted and what materials will be presented as part of the training program. Elements of each lesson plan should include:

- Learning objectives
- Outline of subject content
- Training scope
- Standards
- Main talking points
- Handouts
- Pre- and posttests
- Competencies

Each lesson plan should include the objectives that will be accomplished during the training session. Objectives should include the training scope, standards, and specific outcomes desired during the training session. For example:

- Each participant will develop a complete understanding of the infant abduction procedure followed by security.
- Participants will learn to exhibit listening and leadership skills as part of their training.

Each lesson plan will outline the course material so that the instructor knows what topics to teach as part of the training session. Areas within the training program that are most important or that relate to the specific skills necessary for the training topic should be highlighted within the training outline. The lesson plan should list all of the session materials that will be used during the class, for example, the material booklet, specific reference sheets, and basic items like pens or pencils so students can take notes. All training sessions should contain some form of pre- and posttest evaluation process. Tests can be written, observational, general discussion, essays, or one-on-one verbal evaluation or questioning. Whichever method is used, it should be contained in the lesson plan. All questions and answers should be included in the plan. The lesson plan should also include a list of competencies to be evaluated as part of the testing process. For example, the skills developed in the training curriculum and listed in the lesson plan should be evaluated to determine if the student can demonstrate each skill during the evaluation process.

Included within the lesson plan should be a course syllabus. A syllabus should be created for each specific training session. It should include the date or dates of training and the names of instructors. It should contain the lesson objectives and outline the topics to be covered during the training session. A syllabus is extremely important to regulatory agencies. They determine when, who, and what was taught. Each syllabus should be placed in a book along with the training curriculum and sign-in sheets so that training information is readily available for regulatory review.

General Training Topics

The subjects of study need to be determined before the training program starts. Topics should incorporate the combined job tasks, functions, policy and procedure review, security-specific processes, and general knowledge topics. The training that is required for hospital security officers is extensive and complex. Topics like use of force and customer service are contradictory in nature but must be spelled out so that officers understand when their roles change and how to effectively manage the different situations they may encounter. Training should be conducted annually, teaching each topic in a way that consistently reinforces behaviors that are desired by the institution. Training topics should be determined, in part, by the completed job assessment, along with standard topics that are specific to the healthcare security industry. These standard topics include:

- Use of force
- Crisis intervention
- Use of restraints
- Customer service
- Role of a security guard
- Job duties/functions
- Legal powers and limitations
- Emergency situations
- Communications and public relations
- Access control
- Report writing
- Ethics and conduct
- Blood-borne pathogens/infection control
- HIPAA and regulatory agencies

Other more specialized topics include:

■ CPR/AED (automated external defibrillator)
■ Handling of psychiatric patients
■ Terrorism
■ Investigations
■ Physical security systems
■ Use of handcuffs
■ Use of weapons (pepper spray, batons, etc.)
■ Understanding special needs patients

Security policies, procedures, and processes should be an integral part of the training program. Security staff need to have a thorough understanding of their role within the hospital, and the best way to achieve that goal is through the review of and instruction on all policies and procedures that are pertinent to the security function.

Teaching Methods

Training can be accomplished many different ways. All training methods should be utilized so that the training process can be ongoing and training material can be continuously reinforced. The most consistent and best form of training is classroom-based training, where an instructor is used to present information that is continually reinforced during the training process. Classroom training should be used for new employee orientation, annual in-service training, and the introduction of new materials, like active shooter training, so that officers are provided with the best learning environment and can understand and retain as much information as possible. Classroom training offers the best environment for staff to learn and retain information presented during the training process. Classroom training should include a variety of activities in order to present material. Using various techniques helps to keep the student engaged and increases retention of presented materials. These include lectures by instructors and other persons that have knowledge of or can present on a particular topic. Mixing up speakers is the best way to present material in the lecture format. Having one person continually present is boring and can leave students nonengaged. Bringing in administrators from other hospital departments or peers from other hospitals is one way to mix up the lecture process and help maintain engagement. Using doctors, especially clinical heads of a department, as speakers is a great way for the clinical staff to better understand security and for security to better understand the clinician's role in the healthcare facility. Lecturing should not be the only method for the distribution of material; using videos, holding demonstrations, having group discussions, and conducting role-plays are all methods that can be used to present class material to students. Videos can be an effective tool for presenting educational material. However, they should be used sparingly and should not be presented one after another, but broken up and viewed throughout the training cycle. Demonstration is a way for the lecturer to present material in order to break up the routine of standing in front of the class and speaking. Additionally, many people are visual learners, so demonstration is an effective way to increase student retention. Like demonstrations, group activities are an effective way to help students learn and retain information. One of the best ways for students to retain processes is to utilize role-playing during the training process. Having students stand up in front of the class and act out different processes or scenarios can help the actor and observer better comprehend training material. Methods used during the training process should be part of the training standards so that material is delivered on a consistent basis, and each method used should be listed in the training curriculum.

On-the-Job Training

Once the formal classroom training is completed, on-the-job training should be implemented in order to help new employees get oriented to the hospital and surrounding properties. On-the-job training means having a new employee or newly promoted employee shadow a more experienced staff member in order to see and feel the job firsthand. Every position in the security department should provide on-the-job training for new persons and persons promoted up within the security organization. On-the-job training for new employees should include continued tours and patrols of the entire hospital, review of all officer posts and their procedures, and any processes necessary for the completion of the job. In addition, field training should be part of on-the-job training. That means responding to all calls for service, like door openings, patient restraints, and recording of incident reports. On-the-job training should be conducted immediately after classroom training is completed. This will allow the staff member to see firsthand the practical application of each skill and concept that was reviewed during the formal training process. All tasks conducted for on-the-job training should be included in the training checklist so that all tours, posts, and calls for service instruction are documented.

On-the-job training is also useful when an employee is promoted into a new role, like supervisor, dispatcher, or investigator. As part of the onboarding process, newly promoted employees should have time to orient themselves into their new position. As with a new employee who is orienting into the hospital security department and its culture, a promoted employee should have time to adjust their mindset into their new role and the culture that may exist within that level of the organization. For promoted employees, a formal process should be set up and documented that outlines the on-the-job process and what needs to be accomplished as part of the transition. On-the-job training for promoted employees should be a minimum of two months or two-thirds of the probationary period. This will ensure that the employee has a full understanding of their new position and the processes that are required in order to make them successful.

Training Competencies

An important part of any training program is the creation and implementation of competencies. A competency is a set of behaviors or skills important to a particular job function that can be tested in order to demonstrate that a staff member understands that job function. Competencies provide verification that staff understand and have retained the knowledge presented in formal training. Each training subject or topic should contain a set of competencies so that staff can be evaluated to determine if they have retained and understand key components of the training session.

Competency development starts with the use of the skills outlined within the training curriculum and lesson plan. These skills, along with other information necessary for a staff member to understand their job, will determine the competencies to be evaluated. For example, the skill of neat penmanship would be necessary in order to write incident reports or fill out a logbook. Remembering to have a nurse present during the collection of valuables is an important process in valuables collection and should be evaluated to ensure that staff meet that requirement when collecting valuables.

Competency evaluations come in several different forms: pretraining test, posttraining test, and midpoint training. They can be assessed through either written testing (questions and answers), verbal testing, the demonstration of a skill, or observation of a security process.

Additional Training Methods

There are several alternative methods to train staff that are effective in providing information and training reinforcement. They can be used to continually strengthen previous training or policy and procedure. These techniques should not be used for detailed training or the introduction of new topics or concepts. These methods should only be used to reinforce training presented in the classroom setting.

Mini-Lessons

Mini-lessons are short, consolidated versions of longer training that is reviewed during roll call, breaks, or mealtime in order to highlight important or key aspects of existing training topics, policies and procedures, or security processes. When used on a regular basis, it can consistently reinforce the key skills and job functions related to each policy, procedure, or process. Mini-lessons should be formatted to include the policy statement, a short outline statement summarizing the overall policy or procedure, and specific job functions required by the security officer, supervisor, dispatcher, etc. Mini-lessons should be read to staff in order to provide consistent application of the training process. There can be a large number of mini-lessons incorporated into the training process, enough so that they are repeated only about once a month or every other month. Mini-lessons should be reviewed yearly or when a policy, procedure, or process changes. In addition, lessons should be changed periodically so that information is not redundant and becomes boring. Repeating the same information over and over again only creates a training environment where staff become unengaged. Mini-lessons can also focus on current events in healthcare, review the current emergency preparedness drill that the hospital conducted, or concentrate on areas that management knows need to be improved. Mini-lessons are low cost and are used to reinforce classroom training and focus on required job functions and skills. The disadvantages to using mini-lessons is that they provide no feedback or evaluation of information retention and may not work during meal or break times because staff may be required to be paid for their time.

Computer-Based/Online Training

Computer-based training is completed through a series of videos, PowerPoint presentations, or animated stories presented on a computer screen. They are sometimes interactive, requiring the student to answer questions or respond to presented scenarios. Programs are usually developed by a third party but can be generated in-house with the purchase of specialized software. Persons participating in this kind of training are usually required to answer questions and provide feedback on information that is presented in the training program. Online training can track users, determining right and wrong answers as well as completion dates and times. The advantage to using computer-based training is that users can conduct the training according to their schedule. It does not require a classroom setting. Online training is expensive and does not allow for the answering of any questions related to the training material, and retention rates for this type of training are low.

Midpoint Competency Evaluations

Many trainers use midpoint competency evaluations in order to reinforce prior training. Midpoint evaluations are conducted in order to evaluate training retention and reinforce training not retained during classroom training. Midpoint evaluations are the evaluation of competency halfway through the formal training cycle, the midpoint between the annual classroom training sessions or six months after the completion of new employee orientation training. Midpoint evaluations are conducted as competency-based training and focus on specific job tasks or functions. It is not the content that is important in competency-based evaluation but the process or behaviors of carrying out a specific policy or program. Competency evaluations can be conducted through observation, demonstration, or a written or verbal test. The advantage to using midpoint competency training is that it will help to reinforce existing training and help staff to retain information that they may have forgotten after the formal training process has concluded. Competency training is short, usually 10–15 minutes in duration, so staff are not taken away from their job for too long. It is inexpensive and does provide some measure of feedback to students who might have questions about the evaluation process. Competency evaluations do not allow for the presentation of new information and are not a training refresher. Staff sit down to take a test, are asked to demonstrate a process, or are observed going through a process and scored based on their skill level related to the behavior and skill necessary for them to conduct their job. For example, an observation competency evaluation pertaining to a patient restraint would consist of a review on how a security officer handled the patient. The observation can be conducted during an actual patient restraint, for example, what was said to the patient as the officer approached (de-escalation), how the officer approached the patient for a takedown, the specific techniques used to hold down a patient (hand on the thigh and knee), and how the restraints were applied.

Training Staff

No matter how small or large the security department, there should be one person who is in charge of the training program. The assigned training officer should have some experience with training and spend time to develop and implement the training curriculum, syllabus, etc., before the training program begins. Instructors should be chosen from both inside and outside of the security department. If the hospital has a training department, a member of that team should work great as an instructor as well as act as an adviser to the security department training program. Supervisors and senior management are great choices as instructors, if they have good presentation skills. The advantage to using management as trainers is that they are exposed to the training material, so they know what is being taught. Many times, management review the training program but are not exposed to the training material in a training setting. Management that are not instructing should be students within the class, so that they are exposed and understand the training material.

A mentor or on-the-job trainer program should be part of the training process. This person or persons should be selected in advance at the start of the training program. The process to become a mentor should include a formal request by staff and an interview process for selection. Many times, security departments choose the most senior staff to be mentors for new employees or employees that wish to become management. This may not be the best decision. The best way to engage staff and develop talent is to make the mentor process an important one, choosing the most qualified persons to be in that role.

Mentors should be used with new employees for on-the-job training. During the formal training process, a mentor should be selected to work with a new employee in order to show them the ropes, posts, locations of important departments, patrols, identification of hospital senior management, etc. Each new employee should have an individual mentor, when possible, or a new employee can move from mentor to mentor in order to learn different aspects of the job. A mentor selected for a new employee should stay assigned to the employee for at least the duration of the probationary period. After on-the-job training has been completed, the mentor should meet with the new employee at least once a week in order to answer questions, review training material, and continue to train the new employee on department and hospital processes.

The mentoring process should be used for employees that wish to move up in rank to supervisor, manager, or director. Mentoring at this level can be a person within the security department or from an outside department. Either way, a formal mentoring process should be set up before the process is introduced. Like a training curriculum, a formal written process should be developed. This should include goals and objectives, specific assignments, a meeting timetable, and specific outcomes. This type of program should be monitored by the hospital's training department; if that is not possible, then a senior member of the security department should be assigned to monitor the program and ensure that all objectives, training, and goals are maintained and met. When implemented properly, mentoring is a great way to start employment and arm potential managers with the tools necessary to be successful within the security department or any hospital department.

Evaluation of the Training Program

In order to maintain an effective training program, specific aspects of the program must be evaluated on a regular basis. Evaluation needs to be conducted to determine how staff performed during the training process. Were staff bored? Was the training material to easy or advanced? Were the tests too hard or too easy? Did staff retain the knowledge presented during the training process? Each year the training material must be reviewed to update content. New policies and procedures need to be included, and policies that are changed must be updated. Newly relevant training material needs to be determined each year. Are training topics still relevant and what new topics need to be added? Competencies need to be reviewed to ensure that they are providing the reinforcement necessary for staff to understand and retain the training material they have been taught.

Evaluations should be conducted annually and as a team. The team should consist of the security director and all of the security training staff. In addition, if the institution has a hospital-wide training team, they should be part of the evaluation process. In order to evaluate the effectiveness of the security program, all data related to test scores and competency evaluations should be included. In addition, evaluation sheets should be developed for each class and filled out by each student at the conclusion of the training session. The evaluation should include a rating for:

■ The instructor(s)
■ The class material
■ The teaching methods use
■ The usefulness of the training subject

The evaluation should also include a request for future training topics and any changes that could be made to improve the training process. The evaluation process should include a third-party evaluation of the classroom, a third party who will sit in on the class and evaluate the instructor and observe students to determine their engagement. Classroom evaluations can be conducted using the hospital's training staff or any other trainer outside of the security department. A great alternative to using hospital staff is a local college or university student that would be willing to assist in evaluating the training program.

Data Collection

An effective training program is based on data. Data needs to be collected so that there is a record of completion, outline of what was conducted, and system to evaluate the effectiveness of the training program. Data collection starts with a training checklist. This document provides a list of the training conducted during new employee orientation and annual training. The document lists all training subjects completed and on-the-job training conducted, and contains the dates each training topic was conducted, the trainer's name and signature, and in some cases, the initials of the student. Each student must have their own checklist and the checklist must be placed in the employee's personnel file. The orientation checklist should be kept within the personnel file forever. Annual training records should be kept for at least three years or during the hospital accreditation cycle.

Sign-in sheets should be completed for all training. The sheet should include each student's name, printed out as well as the employee's signature. The sheet should include the time and date for the training session, the instructors' names, and each topic covered during the training process. All tests and other competency evaluations should be collected from the employees and saved for evaluation. Test and evaluation data should be used to evaluate the validity of test questions and the percentage answered correctly and incorrectly. Data analysis for training should include exception analysis: missed due dates, failing scores, and test question percentages answered correctly/incorrectly.

In addition to training data, a yearly timetable should be generated that tracks renewals or continuous education requirements for certification and licensure renewal. License expiration dates should be tracked to ensure that all licensed positions have an active license. Keeping track of this data allows security to remind licensees of their due dates and ensures that they are in compliance with all licensure training requirements.

An Example of a Data-Driven Training Program

In order to increase customer satisfaction at the lobby entrances while developing a screening process that was stringent enough for hospital staff to feel safe, the security department decided to rely on a series of questions to establish an individual's authorization to enter the hospital, slowly decreasing the department's reliance on checking driver's licenses or other types of positive ID. The security department utilized the current hospital patient satisfaction survey and observational competencies to measure the success of the training initiative.

The customer service/screening program was implemented by the security department through the implementation of a hospital-wide generic customer service training program. The program was supported through continual media reinforcement, i.e., posters, written material in current hospital-wide print media, and the creation of a customer service newsletter. The security department utilized its new employee orientation and annual training program to implement the generic customer service training initiative along with the screening initiative. After each customer service training module was completed, training contents were evaluated and reinforced within the department through printed media distributed at each security post, through daily roll call announcements, and through observational competency conducted by supervisors that provided continuous reinforcement of the program principles while the officers were on post.

The hospital-wide customer service program was designed to be implemented over a three-year period introducing one aspect of the program at a time. After implementation of each phase, an evaluation of the phase was conducted, and the next phase was not introduced until collected data indicated that the security officers had changed their culture and were utilizing each phase on a regular basis. The security department incorporated specific aspects of its guest screening program into each component of the hospital's customer service program. Each phase of the program was introduced in a formal classroom setting through lecture and the use of guest speakers from hospital administration. For the first phase of the training, the security department augmented the customer service program by outlining exactly where each officer should stand at each post when greeting guests. After the training was completed, post standing positions were reinforced through roll call reminders and diagrams left at each post. Observational competencies were developed and used monthly in order to evaluate the effectiveness of the positional training. Competency data was used to evaluate the effectiveness of the training . During the next phase of the program, the security department introduced a detailed review of each type of person that enters each specific entrance and reviewed the entry restrictions for each person. For example, at one entrance flower vendors were restricted deliveries had to be announced to the recipient and were only allowed from 8:00 a.m. to 5:00 p.m., Monday through Friday. A written test was used to validate the training process, and then roll call reminders, written post orders, and observational competencies were used to evaluate the effectiveness of the initial and roll call training process.

During the third phase of the customer service training initiative, the security department introduced the officers to "scripting." Scripting is a finite set of phrases or sentences used by the security officers as a standard greeting and to determine a guest's purpose for entering the facility. It provides consistency throughout the department and shifts in the greeting utilized among officers. During this phase of the training, post training was used to reinforce the initial training process on scripting. Then observational competencies were used to collect data on scripting's effectiveness. During the scripting process, a series of questions were presented to the security staff to use in order to determine the necessity of visitation after hospital visiting hours ended. For the next customer service initiative, security staff were trained on scripted questioning of all persons entering the facility during all hours of the day and night. At this point, questioning replaced the use of presenting positive ID.

In the last phase of the customer service training program, a review was conducted of the entire program. Going forward, roll call reminders and competency observational checks were used to gather data to see how the program was progressing. In addition, new employee orientation and annual training included an overview of the program and specific aspects of each phase.

As a result of this initiative, customer service scores increased by an average of 4% per year over the three-year implementation of the program. In addition to asking questions, an additional resource was added to the customer service aspect of the program: security staff provided visitors with detailed directions on where they had to go as part of the screening process. For those persons who did not know where they were going, the customer service/screening process helped to determine their purpose and provided them with directions to their destination.

Chapter 4

Proactive Crime Prevention

Introduction

In order to provide more value to the healthcare organization, the security department needs to focus on the prevention of crime. Hospital crime prevention is about identifying criminal activity and implementing fixes before more crime can occur, rather than reacting to crimes as they occur. Today's crime prevention has evolved; it is about predicting incidents before they occur in a quantifiable way, a way in which hospital administrators can understand and relate too. In order for a security department to migrate to this strategy, relevant data must be collected and analyzed in order to identify trends and recognize emerging patterns in criminal behavior so that proven resolutions can be instituted that will prevent future incidents. Crime prevention began with a police officer walking the beat, patrolling a neighborhood attempting to resolve social problems within the neighborhood they served. These services later extended to educating the community on crime reduction and developing crime prevention surveys for businesses and residences. Today, crime prevention has become more scientific. Criminologists have conducted studies that have resulted in quantifiable measures that reduce and even predict crime.

Leading Research

A growing number of criminologists rooted in scientific methodology have developed approaches for preventing and predicting crime. These theorists use "evidence-based" modeling to quantify the effectiveness of their crime prevention theories. These theories identify criminal activity, predict future activity, and track criminal behavior through trending and pattern recognition. Five theories clarify the best methods in the identification, prediction, and prevention of crime and can be utilized for both the public and private sectors. These methods are "hot spots," "mapping," recidivism of offender and victim, broken windows, and crime prevention through environmental design (CPTED). All five of these models contribute elements necessary for a proactive, high-quality, comprehensive crime prevention strategy.

Hot Spot Theory

In 1986, the Minneapolis, Minnesota, Police Department began an experiment testing the effect of police presence on crime. The Minneapolis experiment concluded that crime is clustered in small areas, or hot spots. These hot spots accounted for the majority of crime and disorder within the city of Minneapolis. The study, which analyzed 323,000 calls to the police, concluded that a small number of hot spots produced most of the crime in the city. Specifically, 3.5% of designated street addresses produced 50% of the calls where police were dispatched. This concentration was even greater for crimes like robbery, criminal sexual conduct, and auto theft, where only 5% of the 115,000 street addresses and intersections in Minneapolis produced 100% of those calls.[1] A similar study conducted in Jersey City, New Jersey, looked at drug crimes and determined that about 4% of addresses and intersections generated half of the city's narcotics arrests and 42% of the disorder arrests.[2]

Many police agencies have concluded, since the publication of these studies, that place-based policing as opposed to person-based policing is more efficient in preventing crime. A recent Police Foundation report indicated that 7 out of 10 police departments use some form of the hot spot modeling to reduce crime and obtained significant crime reduction within the designated hot spot areas by utilizing directed patrols, proactive arrests, and problem-oriented policing. Additionally, the report found that many police departments use civil remedies to reduce crime in hot spots by persuading area residents to take responsibility and action to prevent and reduce crime within their neighborhoods, also known as the broken windows theory. Research shows that hot spot crime prevention can reduce crime without increasing crime in adjacent areas and that crime depends not just on criminals and policing in key places but also on other factors, such as fences, alleys, and other environmental features.[3]

Crime Mapping

Mapping is similar to the hot spot theory. Mapping of crime locations and other variables allows for the tracking and trending of incident data to react to incident rates. With the advent of desktop computers, the idea of hot spots for crime analysis allows for the tracking of variables specific to individual incidents or crimes. Through incident location analysis, crimes are analyzed to identify specific areas to reduce crime and predict future occurrence locations. In addition to locations, time of day, day of the week, or incident type can be mapped on a computer to determine relationships with each other and other variables collected in incident or crime reports. As an example, studies suggest that crime and public disorder tend to concentrate at certain times of the day or day of the week. Assaults, for example, occur most frequently between 3:00 a.m. and 7:00 a.m. when streets are vacant. Residential burglaries mostly occur during daytime hours when residents are not home. Incidents of driving under the influence occur more frequently in areas with a large number of bars or liquor stores. Through incident analysis, predictions can be made as to where, when, or what types of crimes will occur, allowing police departments to more efficiently deploy resources in order to reduce criminal activity.[4]

Repeat Offender and Victim

In 1986, because too little money was available for police to protect all of the homes and businesses within their districts, police in England focused on and studied the homes and businesses that were determined to be most at risk. Their study examined burglary data and determined that there were a significant number of repeat victims for these crimes. Their study concluded that the best predictor of a future burglary was past burglary. The same is true for victimization. Studies again showed that an individual's past crime victimizations are a good predictor of subsequent victimization. These patterns in crime occur for two reasons. The first is the assessment of risk by the offender. For example, a house on a busy street within a poor neighborhood is less likely to be victimized than a house that is in an isolated location and in the middle of a high-income neighborhood. The second reason is that victims make a repeat occurrence more likely. A burglar walking down a street for the first time sees houses that he considers suitable and unsuitable targets. If he successfully burglarizes one home, the next time he walks down that same street he knows one home that is a suitable target because he remembers his way in and out and what items are inside. Studies that interviewed incarcerated burglars, robbers, and victims back up the repeat victimization theory. Additionally, studies related to cleared crimes support repeat victimization. These studies also found that the greater the number of prior victimizations, the higher the probability that the victim will experience a future crime, especially within crime-prone neighborhoods. When victimization does recur, it does so very soon after the prior occurrence and usually with the same perpetrator(s). These studies confirm that if you want to predict crime or prevent future crimes, a good place to look is at past victims and prior offenders.[5]

Crime Prevention through Environmental Design

The idea that environmental design might play a role in crime reduction had its roots in Jane Jacobs's book *The Life and Death of Great American Cities* (1961). Using personal observation and description, Jacobs's book suggests that residential crime could be reduced by orienting buildings toward the street, clearly distinguishing between public and private domains, and placing outdoor spaces in proximity to frequently used areas. In 1971, architect Oscar Newman published a paper entitled "Architectural Design for Crime Prevention," and in 1973 he published a book, *Defensible Space, Crime Prevention through Urban Design*. Like Jacobs, Newman identified human territoriality, natural surveillance, and the modification of existing structures as ways to reduce crime. His studies of public housing projects demonstrated how the physical design of buildings contributed to victimization. He determined that their design and location created an environment where no one cared about the place where they lived. The design made it difficult to determine residents from intruders. The idea behind the defensible space theory is to focus on the physical layout of buildings to allow residents control of their living areas. This includes not only the building lobbies and corridors but also the streets and grounds outside of them. Newman's work became the foundation for what is known today as CPTED.

The term "crime prevention through environmental design" first appeared in a 1971 book by criminologist and sociologist C. Ray Jeffery. Inspired by Jacobs's work, Jeffrey analyzed the causation of crime from several different approaches: criminal law, several models of crime control, the administration of justice, criminology, and penology. He also drew from fields outside of criminal justice, like systems analysis, decision theory, environmentalism, behaviorism, sociology, and psychology. Jeffery went on to make the general argument that crime prevention should focus on factors related to the biology of crime, such as exposure to lead, which he thought caused brain damage and delinquency in children, and to reducing the environmental opportunities for crime. However, his book contained few practical applications for reducing crime. A follower of Jeffery, Tim Crowe, in 1991 expanded on Jeffery's work and developed a comprehensive set of guidelines to reducing opportunities for crime in the built environment. His work was published as a guide for police, town planners, and architects in preventing crime.

CPTED is based on one simple principle: crime is opportunity based and opportunities are created through the physical environment. By altering environmental opportunities, crime can be reduced. This includes crimes like airline hijackings, white-collar crime, obscene phone calls, violence, and domestic violence, as well as property crimes. CPTED is based on four basic premises: territorial control, access control, natural surveillance, and image and maintenance. Territorial and access control consist of virtual and actual barriers that reduce the opportunity for criminals to commit crime. CPTED looks to utilize natural strategies to decrease opportunities by denying access to targets and creating a perception of risk in offenders. Access control utilizes mechanical concepts like devices and technology that make committing the crime more difficult. Sometimes referred to as "target hardening," mechanical measures emphasize hardware and technological systems, such as locks, security screens on windows, fencing and gating, key control systems, closed-circuit television (CCTV), and other security technologies. Windows may have protective glazing that withstands blows without breaking. Doors and window hardware may have special material and mountings that make them hard to remove or tamper with. Walls, floors, or doors may be specially reinforced in high-security areas with materials that are difficult to penetrate.

Natural surveillance is intended to make intruders easily observable through increased awareness by building users. CPTED utilizes building features to create a sense of ownership by users so that offenders perceive territorial influence and surveillance. Natural surveillance strategies maximize the visibility of people, parking areas, and building entrances. Examples are doors and windows that look onto streets and parking areas, pedestrian-friendly sidewalks and streets, front porches, and adequate nighttime lighting. Natural surveillance also includes organizational concepts, which rely on people to provide surveillance and access control functions. Organizational concepts include concierges, security guards, designated guardians, residents in Neighborhood Watch programs, police officer patrols, and other individuals with the ability to observe, report, and intervene in undesirable or illegitimate actions.

Image and maintenance means changing the design of streets, sidewalks, building entrances, and neighborhood gateways by use of architectural and landscape structural elements to discourage access to private areas. These concepts employ physical and spatial features such as site and architectural elements to ensure that a setting acts as a deterrent to crime while supporting the intended use of the space, for example, features such as landscape planting, pavement surface design, gateway treatments, and fences that define property lines and help distinguish private from public spaces. Continual maintenance of the buildings and spaces denotes ownership of property. When there is no ownership, areas tend to deteriorate, creating a greater tolerance of disorder. An article published in 1982 by social scientists James Q. Wilson and George L. Kelling explains this idea. Their theory, broken windows, supports a zero-tolerance approach to property maintenance, demonstrated by the presence of a broken window in a building that entices vandals to break more windows in the vicinity. This creates an overall impression that the area or property has no ownership, which increases the probability of crime. Ownership creates a positive image in the community by showing a sense of pride and self-worth. The upkeep of an area demonstrates that someone cares and is watching. For example, the sooner broken windows are fixed, the less likely it is that such vandalism will occur in the future.[6]

The Development of a Crime Prevention Program

Crime prevention in healthcare, as in law enforcement, works best using an evidence-based model; the proven methods discussed above reduce crime and even predict crime before it occurs. Mapping generates data that identifies the highest-frequency crime areas or hot spots. Hot spots can be analyzed further to develop trends and patterns within the hot spot areas. This data, along with data that analyzes victim and offender demographics, creates definitive, predictable trends in crime that can be resolved through security solutions that include strategies like CPTED, directed patrol, and security surveys.

In 1993, a study entitled "Situation Crime Prevention Used in an Urban Hospital Setting" demonstrated that mapping and hot spots reduced crime in a hospital setting. This study determined that the majority of crime was committed in one area of the hospital. In this study, the area with the highest crime was the emergency department. Further analysis of the emergency department crime data determined the most frequent time and date of occurrence, allowing the security department to provide directed patrols, reducing crime in the defined hot spot area. The identification of problem areas allowed the security department to attack the highest concentrations of crime using a systematic, well-planned approach. The study utilized the techniques discussed above to analyze crime and determine its most prevalent hot spots based on location, time, and victim characteristics.

Identification of Trends and Patterns

Mapping data allows for the identification and resolution of crime in the healthcare setting. The first step in the creation of an effective crime prevention program is the collection of relevant crime and activity data so that mapping can occur. The data most helpful in the identification of crime is incident report and call for service data. Incident report and call for service data can help to determine crime locations, the time of day that crime occurs, the type of crime occurring, the day of the week that crimes occur, and the patients, visitors, and staff who are most likely to be victims. Security departments respond to many different types of calls. Those calls that are specific to unauthorized persons and suspicious and unusual activity, like doors found open, if not captured in an incident report, should be included in the crime prevention data collection. Basic data that should be collected includes:

- Incident type
- Location—Building, floor, room number, and hospital service (department)
- Time—Day of the week, month of year, time of day or shift
- Victim—Sex, age, status (visitor, employee, etc.)

The collected data should be entered into a spreadsheet program like Excel. Data should be collected and entered on a daily basis. For security departments that have a lower volume of data, data can be entered on

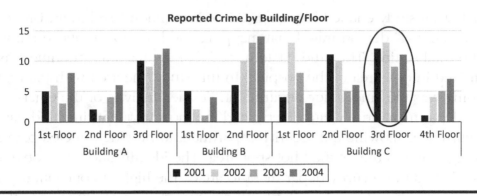

Figure 4.1 Example of date frequency by location.

a weekly or biweekly schedule. The reason for placing data in a spreadsheet is to determine the highest frequency of events. Identifying the frequency of events is the prime attribute in the determination of hot spots. Remember, hot spots represent the highest frequency of events within the data category. Over time, depending on the number of data points, specific patterns in frequency will start to emerge. As patterns or trends begin to materialize, problem areas present themselves. For example, in the study listed above, location date indicated that the highest frequency for location within the incident report data was the emergency department. As demonstrated in Figure 4.1, data frequency provides a clear picture of high-crime areas.

Hot Spot Identification and Detailed Analysis

Once hot spots have been identified, the next step in crime reduction is the analysis of collected data specific to the hot spot areas. A more thorough analysis of high-frequency variables for that data set or area will help to identify reasons for crimes being committed in the hot spot areas. A deeper drive into the patterned or trending data will determine variables that when addressed will reduce crime. Incident reports and call for service data specific to identified hot spot areas or demographics should be collected and analyzed to determine further trends in time of day, type of calls or incidents, day of the week, victim and perpetrator names, or any other trends that are observed in the data review. For example, in the study on hospital hot spots, the highest-incident locations were determined to be in the emergency department, followed by several clinics and inpatient units. For the study, all of the incident reports and logbook entries for the emergency department were separated and reviewed individually. This review determined specific patterns that accounted for the high volume of reports generated in this area. A closer examination determined that the highest-volume area within the emergency department was the waiting area and the highest-frequency crime category was disorderly conduct. Additionally, it was determined that the majority of the disorderly conduct summons were issued to a small number of the same patients. The result of this analysis provided quantitative evidence that security resources within the emergency department waiting area should be greater, and crime reduction within the waiting area was reduced through the identification of and dealing with the repeat disorderly conduct offenders.[7]

Identifying Solutions to Reduce Crime

Through research and experience, police departments have found scientifically based solutions to reducing crime, strategies that provide verifiable reductions in the rate of crime. These strategies include directed patrols, problem-oriented policing, CPTED, Neighborhood Watch programs, victim and offender tracking, awareness training, and security surveys. These same methods can work in the healthcare setting. When properly implemented, these crime reduction methods can help to reduce the level of crime within the healthcare setting.

Directed Patrol

Directed patrol is a great preventer of crime as proven in hot spot studies. Directed patrol in the healthcare setting includes patrols of the interior and exterior of the hospital based on incident data collected on the time and day of incident occurrence. Even though the precise time and day of occurrence are not always available or accurate, this data should still be collected and analyzed to determine possible crime or incident occurrences. Officers should patrol hot spot locations during the times and days where crime is committed most frequently. As crime patterns and trends change or shift to other areas, patrols should be modified to meet those trends. The presence of a security officer helps to prevent crime and identify possible future criminal activity.

Directed patrolling is not only about visibility or walking through an area during times of occurrence; officers patrolling hot spot areas should have a very specific purpose. Data related to the potential cause of the crime trend in the hot spot areas should be collected and reviewed to determine key characteristics related to the incidents occurring in the hot spot area. Demographic data can determine descriptions of potential offenders, offices, or areas that have been hit repeatedly, and this data should be communicated to patrol personnel on a regular basis, so as data trends change officers can look for those distinguishing factors while on patrol. Officers conducting directed patrols should be trained to look for individuals that have been identified as offenders, or visitors or staff that have been victims. Officers should also be trained on basic crime prevention techniques, for example, identifying doors left unlocked and personal items unattended or any other unusual activity. While on patrol, officers should look to close and lock doors, and make patients, visitors, and staff lock up valuables.

Neighborhood Watch Program

Neighborhood Watch programs are also a useful strategy to reduce crime. Neighborhood Watch programs consist of education and programming that make residents more aware of crime prevention techniques and promote accountability to public spaces. Developed out of the broken windows theory, the Neighborhood Watch concept teaches residents to develop a personal stake in their neighborhood in order to reduce crime. According to the broken windows theory, when residents take a personal stake in their neighborhood, keep it clean and vandal-free, and monitor public areas, i.e., call police when they see suspicious activity, crime is reduced. The Neighborhood Watch concept works best when connected with other programs that create community responsibility and social activity, encouraging residents to take responsibility for public areas and their neighborhood environment. This increases the overall surveillance capacity and resident's responsibility for their community. The concept of Neighborhood Watch can work in the hospital environment as well. When employees take a personal stake in their work areas, are aware of patients and visitors, keep an eye out for unauthorized persons, and make sure that patient property, as well as their own, is properly secured, crime within their work area will be reduced. In healthcare, staff can decorate their units for the holidays, have activities that involve the patients and visitors, perform daily rounding, and conduct huddles, which will increase staff dedication to their work area while increasing their situational awareness. Programs like these promote awareness and can reduce the amount of crime that occurs within a specific unit or floor, and even throughout the entire healthcare facility.

Incorporating CPTED into the Security Program

As described earlier, CPTED techniques need to be incorporated into all aspects of security services and institutional design. They should be part of all security surveys. They are useful when designing or renovating areas and should be a standard part of any construction project. They need to be utilized any time physical security systems are being installed, like CCTV and access control or physical barriers like doors, partitions, or fencing. In healthcare, the most important concept of the CPTED model is the use of target hardening and surveillance capacity. Target hardening is the creation of barrier layers that restrict access in order to reduce the opportunity to commit a crime. Surveillance capacity is the design and construction of areas so that employees can visually monitor their work area. An example of target hardening would be the installation of lockers with locks or providing keys to desk draws for employees to secure their valuables while at work. Installing safes in patient rooms for the security of their valuables or installing dead bolt locks on doors that contain valuable equipment are other examples. Additionally, installing lockers in a locked room provides further hardening, requiring potential thieves to break into both the room and the lockers to obtain personal items.

Surveillance capacity or situational awareness refers to the ability of staff to visually monitor patients and visitors, as well as other staff. Surveillance can be live, in person, or remote via CCTV. Either way, it is important for staff to be able to see what is going on around them. When designing or renovating areas within the hospital, it is important to consider surveillance capacity for staff as well as patients. Examples of increased surveillance capacity include window panels installed in fire doors so that staff can see what is going on on the other side of closed doors. Lowering the nursing station walls so that nurses can see all activity in the hallways around them, the installation of CCTV in isolated areas like waiting rooms so that activities can be monitored, and the installation of mirrors in hallways so that staff can see around hallway corners are other examples.

Victim and Offender Tracking

Identifying and tracking victims and offenders is another technique that can be useful in reducing crime. When combined with opportunity reduction programs like directed patrol, watch programs, and CPTED, the identification and tracking of offenders and victims can help to reduce crime. Like location and time of day analysis, tracking the names of victims and offenders allows for the identification of trends in victimization. Part of data analysis or the mapping process should include both victim and offender name frequency. Names should be gathered as part of incident reporting or call for service data in order to track their involvement with crimes or potential criminal acts. Names should be collected and analyzed for all victims, offenders, and witnesses, even for service calls related to security activities like doors found open or unlocked, or staff missing keys or needing a door opened. All contribute to data that helps to identify trends in potential crime.

The use of "BOLOS" (be on the lookout for) is helpful in the identification of offenders that may be active within a specific hot spot area. BOLOs are printed or digital photos of potential offenders with basic information about them and their activities in order to educate persons residing in hot spot areas on the potential offender's description. Posting pictures and general information on suspected or known offenders helps staff to quickly identify repeat offenders and helps to increase the staff's situational awareness. BOLOs are only effective in the prevention of crime when used properly. In order to ensure compliance with HIPAA regulations, photos and demographic information should be treated as confidential, unless the data is coming from law enforcement, in which case it is considered public information. BOLO distribution should be restricted to only hot spot areas and to those persons that are in a position to identify the offender. BOLOs should never be posted in public areas, which include staff break or locker rooms and nurses' stations. BOLOs should be kept in a binder so that they are covered at all times and should be viewed by staff during meetings/huddles or when staff are on break. BOLO information should be kept in a nonpublic area where the binder can be secured behind a locked door, for example, a break room or supervisor's work office. When the individual listed in a BOLO is caught, all of the BOLOs should be collected by security and destroyed. A single copy should be kept by security for potential future use.

When offenders are caught, studies indicate that arrest is a strong deterrent for the commission of future crimes. Getting caught decreases recidivism only when there is a punishment associated with it. Many institutions, including healthcare, escort offenders out of the door after signing a document admitting their offense and agreeing not to return. This process is ineffective in reducing repeat offender activity. Healthcare institutions should arrest all apprehended offenders, whether patients or visitors, for their first and any additional offenses committed on hospital property. This policy will dramatically reduce the potential for future crimes and repeat victimization.

Awareness Programming

Awareness training or education is a common practice in crime prevention programming. Providing educational materials to healthcare staff on crime prevention helps the hospital and staff to promote crime reduction, personal safety, and situational awareness. Whether developed in-house or from a third party, education and training should be a major part of the crime prevention program. General crime prevention training should be part of new employee orientation as well as yearly in-service training. Specialized training programs should be developed for hot spot areas to educated staff, patients, and visitors on the risks associated with the crime trends occurring within the hot spot areas.

Crime prevention educational programs can be developed either through in-house sources like public relations, from third-party companies like the National Crime Prevention Council, or through police and law enforcement agencies. Awareness programs can be general in nature and educate staff, patients, and visitors on general crime prevention or can be specialized based on the season or patterns occurring within the healthcare facility, customized to provide awareness during high-crime times like holidays, vacation periods, or as determined through incident analysis. For example, home break-ins occur more frequently during the summer months when people are on vacation and muggings occur more frequently during the Christmas season when people are doing more shopping.

Educational material can be found in many places and address many crime-related issues. The best-known organization is the National Crime Prevention Council (NCPC), which has provided decades of educational materials and programming in crime prevention throughout the United States.

The NCPC was founded in 1982 to manage the National Citizens' Crime Prevention Campaign, McGruff the Crime Dog, and to administer the Crime Prevention Coalition of America. The best-known campaign developed by NCPC is McGruff the Crime Dog. McGruff is an anthropomorphic cartoon bloodhound created by Saatchi & Saatchi through the Ad Council for the National Crime Prevention Council for use by American police in building crime awareness. The NCPC produces tools on crime prevention strategies that include publications and teaching materials on a variety of topics, crime prevention programs, and programs that can be implemented in communities and institutions. Other federal and state organizations provide crime reduction awareness programs addressing specific topics. For example, the Federal Trade Commission offers educational information on identity theft, and the FBI offers prevention programming on violent crimes. Many state and local law enforcement agencies provide crime prevention programming information as well.[8]

Security Survey

The security survey is a tool that is important in the prevention of crime. It helps in the reduction of crime by assessing risk and identifying potential threats and vulnerabilities within hot spot areas. A complete and thorough security survey identifies assets to be protected, determines threats and vulnerabilities, pinpoints areas for improvement, and helps in the development of recommendations to reduce crime. When a hot spot is identified and a detailed data analysis within the hot spot is completed, a security survey should be conducted to determine security improvement within the hot spot area.

References

1. Sherman, Lawrence W. hot spots of crime and criminal careers of place. In John E. Eck and David Weisburg, Eds., *Crime and Place: Crime Prevention Studies*. Vol. 1. New York: National Institute of Justice to the Crime Control Institute, 1995.
2. National Institute of Justice. Hot spot policing can reduce crime. October 14, 2009. https://www.nij.gov/topics/law-enforcement/strategies/hot-spot-policing/pages/welcome.aspx.

3. BragaAnthony A., Andrew V. Papachristos, and David M. Hureau. *Crime Prevention Research Review: Police Programs to Prevent Crime in Hot Spot Areas*. Washington, DC: Community Oriented Policing Services, U.S. Department of Justice, September 2012.

4. *Mapping Out Crime: Providing 21st Century Tools for Safe Communities*. Report of the Task Force on Crime Mapping and Data-Driven Management. Washington, DC: U.S. Department of Justice, National Partnership for Reinventing Government, July 12, 1999.

5. PeaseKen, and Gloria Laycock. *Research in Action, Revictimization: Reducing the Heat of Hot Victims*. NCJ 162951. Washington, DC: National Institute of Justice, November 1996.

6. Clarke, Ronald. *The Theory of Crime Prevention through Environmental Design. Defensible Space and CPTED: Origins and Applications*. https://pdfs. semanticscholar.org/4a94/e72074e829aba49ff001e177870d37be13d5.pdf.

7. Scaglione, Bernard J. Situational crime prevention used in an urban hospital setting. *Security Journal*, Vol. 4, No. 2, 87–96, 1993.

8. National Crime Prevention Council. *About NCPC*. www.ncpc.org/about-ncpc/.

Chapter 5

Incident and Event Investigation

Introduction

Regulatory agencies like the Joint Commission and Occupational Safety and Health Administration (OSHA) mandate that hospitals collect incident report data related to crime and violence to improve processes so that future occurrences can be reduced. From a personal item missing on someone's desk to incidents of workplace violence, all hospital security departments should have a group or individual within their organization that provides investigative services. Investigations are a vital part of the data collection process for security and should be considered part of the hospital's overall process improvement program. Investigations identify victim and perpetrator recidivism and track modus operandi. They dramatically increase the probability of catching perpetrators and returning lost or stolen personal property to victims. Having an investigative process in place within the security department provides customer satisfaction to patients and visitors and promotes positive public relations through investigator interaction with victims, demonstrating the hospital's concern for their property and well-being.

Characteristics of a Successful Investigation

Workplace investigations are defined as a determination of the facts to make a workplace decision or to obtain the facts so that resolution of a complaint and situation can be achieved. In healthcare, the purpose of the investigation function is also to collect characteristic data about events relating to lost, missing, or stolen property; workplace violence; human resource matters; and all general crimes that have been committed within the hospital facility. The key to any successful investigation and reduction of crime is the accurate and timely collection of information related to a reported incident or event. In the world of investigations, timeliness is most important. Over the long term, memories fade and facts tend to be forgotten, so information must be collected immediately upon notification that an incident has occurred. In the healthcare environment, timeliness is even more critical since length of stay is decreasing and patients and visitors may only be on site at the time of the incident and may never be in the hospital again. Information gathered during an investigation should be collected in detail, and the details of the event should be corroborated using primary sources to confirm the data, so information is accurate and complete. Information must be collected in an unbiased manner without offering or pursuing an opinion. An investigator's job is to collect the facts and verify information, not impose personal bias or opinion.

Investigative reports need to be concise and clear. The documentation of an investigation or event can be the determining factor in the outcome of a lawsuit, criminal case, or insurance claim. Reports should state the facts in clear, short sentences written in chronological order. Reports need to be neat, clear, and thorough. They need to provide detailed accounts of what occurred, indicate the evidence collected, and contain the names of all persons involved in the incident. The report should contain not only the names of victims, witnesses, and perpetrators but also their full address, contact information, complete physical description including any unusual markings, and complete statements about the incident.

The interview process is the most important component to a sound investigation; however, the art of the interview is often forgotten. Correct questioning techniques can lead to the discovery of pertinent information important in the investigative process. All persons involved in an incident or crime should be interviewed and six fundamental questions asked to collect detailed information necessary for a complete and thorough investigation. These six basic questions are:

- What occurred?
- Who was involved in the incident?
- When did the incident occur?
- Where did the incident occur?

- How did the incident occur?
- Why did the incident occur?

An investigator should ask these six questions to every interviewee during every interview they conduct. Remember, the thorough collection of information is key to the successful conclusion of any investigation.

Every interview should begin by establishing a baseline of information. This is accomplished by asking simple, easy-to-answer questions such as "What is your name?" "How long have you worked at the company?" Avoid questions that can be answered with a plain yes or no. Then the six fundamental questions should be asked. The investigator should formulate follow-up questions based on the answers provided to the six fundamental questions until a thorough picture is obtained of the incident or event. It helps to ask open-ended questions to get the subject to freely talk about the incident, such as "Tell me about ...."

Avoid loaded questions like "What was your involvement in this incident?" During the interview process, remember that listening is more important than questioning.

The collection and maintenance of evidence is vital to the hospital investigative process. Evidence must be collected correctly if it is going to be used as part of an investigation. The investigator should always carry latex or rubber gloves, self-sealing plastic bags, tape, and a permanent marker when collecting evidence. All evidence should be placed in self-sealing plastic bags. Once a bag is used, it must be marked and sealed. Mark the bag with the date, the time, the investigator's name, a description of the item, the location at which the item was found, and any case or investigation number. The person who collects the evidence should bag it, mark it, and secure it (to maintain a proper chain of evidence), and then place the bag(s) in a secure location. For example, if a screwdriver is found on the floor where a door was forced open, the screwdriver may have been used to open the door. Pry marks found around the lock would confirm that the screwdriver was used in the break-in. The screwdriver may provide ownership through fingerprint evidence or by make and model. The investigator should put on latex gloves and pick up the screwdriver by the middle of its shaft and place it into a self-sealing plastic bag. Wearing gloves and handling the screwdriver in the middle of the shaft will reduce the opportunity to smudge fingerprints on the handle or shaft. Anything found at the scene of the incident should be categorized as evidence until a full picture of the occurrence is obtained. Any items, including items that are normally found within the crime scene area, should be categorized as evidence if it is determined through the investigative process that the item may have been involved in the incident.

Pictures and video are of utmost importance to a hospital investigation. Photos or video should be taken of every incident or event. They are the best representation of an incident or event and can help immensely when reviewing a case years later. Potential lawsuits or court cases resulting from an incident can drag on for years, while memories can fade. An average investigation requires at least four kinds or classifications of photos or video clips. Pictures of the general incident scene (distance shot of the entire incident area) should be taken first. These photos should describe the overall area in which the incident occurred and be limited to two or three photos. Each photo should show the overall incident area from different angles. Then, the scope of the photos should be narrowed to the specific incident area, like the entry door that was broken into or the specific area in the room where the assault occurred. These photos should include not only the specific area of the incident or event but also landmarks so that the photo can be recognized as part of the general incident. These photos should include door numbers, wall hangings, or any other items that will help to determine the location of the incident. The next group of photos should include any evidence found at the scene, and any injuries sustained by victim(s), witnesses, or perpetrator(s). A photo showing the injuries should be in the form of a close-up of the injury, along with a picture of the individual's full body. The full-body picture should include the face and demonstrate the location of the injury on the body.

Conducting the Investigation

The first task for the investigator is to make a list of all persons involved in the incident: witnesses, victims, and perpetrators. The list should include names, addresses, phone numbers, and status (victim, witness, or perpetrator). This list is created first so that all individuals involved in the incident are identified and can be reached in the event that they leave before being interviewed. Remember that the investigator's goal is to obtain statements from everyone immediately after the incident, before they leave. Contacting witnesses and victims by phone, at a later date, can be difficult, especially if the incident results in a criminal case or lawsuit. Once the list is completed, the investigator should obtain statements from all those involved. Statements should be obtained from the witnesses first, since they are the ones to most likely leave first. Make sure anyone in the area of the incident is contacted and asked to make a statement, even if they claim to have seen nothing. The victim should be questioned next, followed by the perpetrator, if one is apprehended. Photos of the incident scene should be taken after statements are obtained. Make sure that injury photos are taken of the victim first. Then photos should be taken of the incident area and any evidence. Physical evidence should be collected and processed last. All of the information collected should be placed in a folder and a formal report should be completed. The report, statements, photos, and evidence should be filed for future use. If a crime has been committed, the police should be notified, depending on the hospital's policy. They are best equipped to locate and follow up with witnesses, victims, and the perpetrator once they have left the facility. The names and badge numbers of the responding police officers should be included in the written report in the event that they need to be contacted in the future.

An accident is defined as a mishap occurring to a person, a vehicle, or both. Liability resulting from an accident can be costly, depending on the circumstances of the event. Slips and falls are the prominent type of accidents encountered in hospitals. They include falls caused by damaged sidewalks or streets, slips on snow and ice, trips up and down stairs, and more commonly, slips on wet floors. As with incident investigations, an accident investigation must start immediately after the accident occurs. It is important to obtain statements from all parties involved and take pictures of the accident before the witnesses, victims, perpetrators, and vehicles leave. As in an incident investigation, a list should be made of the participants: witnesses, victims, and perpetrators. Next, the investigator should obtain statements from all persons involved or who have witnessed the accident. In a vehicle accident investigation, it is important to obtain the driver's license, the vehicle's registration, and insurance information of all drivers and vehicles involved. A detailed drawing of the accident should be completed. This drawing should outline:

- The demographics of the accident area, noting north, east, south, and west
- All landmarks, traffic signs, or traffic lights
- The direction of traffic flow
- The exact location of the vehicle(s) involved
- The direction the involved vehicle(s) was traveling
- The exact location of all damage to the vehicle(s)

Photos should be taken of the accident, like in an incident investigation. Pictures should be taken of the general accident area, and then the victim's injuries and the damage inflicted on the vehicles. In both cases, make sure close-up photos are taken for the personal injury and the property damage. Make sure all of the damage sustained to the vehicle(s) as a result of the accident is photographed. Pictures should include evidence of the accident's cause (skid marks, paint marks on the vehicles or posts, etc.). Drawings, photos, statements, and a formal report should be filed together and stored for future reference. In all accident cases, the police should be notified. As in an incident investigation, the police are in a better position to follow up with victims, witnesses, and perpetrators after all parties leave. In addition, the persons involved in the accident may need a police report for any insurance claim.[1]

Team Approach to Investigations

When starting an investigation program, the security department should create an investigative team. An investigative team is important to the success of the investigative process; it helps to focus and navigate the investigation process, keeping it on track and within process guidelines. It provides legal guidance, ensures compliance with hospital rules and regulations, and ensures compliance with union contacts. The team is also a recommendation resource; it can analyze data to reduce repeat incidents and advise the investigation team on recommendations for changes in the security of the affected area or department. The investigative team members should consist of one member each from human resources, the legal department, compliance, and security. Security department members should include the lead investigator, the physical security specialist, crime prevention, and a member of the security department leadership. The team should meet on a regular basis, depending on investigative workload, and review all investigations in order to recommend investigative direction and potential resolutions.

Data Collection

The collection and analysis of data is important to the security department's continuous quality improvement process. Victim and offender demographics, along with location of occurrence, property types, day and time of day data, help to determine patterns in crime locations, the time of day that crime occurs, the type of crime occurring, the day of the week crimes occur, and patients, visitors, and staff that are most likely to be victims. It is the investigator's job to ensure the viability of information so that crime prevention activities are focused on the correct places and times and with the correct population. For example, names should be gathered as part of the investigative process in order to track their involvement with crimes or potential criminal acts. This data should be analyzed as part of the crime prevention process. Investigations and crime prevention, working together, can dramatically reduce crime within the hospital environment.

The security department's crime prevention efforts can only be successful when accurate and timely data is gathered so that the security department can determine patterns and trends. In order to achieve success, data gathered through investigations needs to be not only accurate, but also consistent. This means that spelling needs to be checked so that names and addresses are accurate; dates and times of occurrence need to be verified so that accurate pattern analysis can occur. The best way to obtain accurate information is to provide preassigned information to the officer or investigator making the report. Today, most electronic incident report software provides drop-down windows with preassigned information for just that reason. If that feature is available, it should be utilized. In order for data analysis to occur, all of the data collected must be consistent. When electronic incident reporting is not available, a written incident report should limit the amount of free text by providing checklists or labeled boxes that request specific information to be obtained in order to complete the report. For better accuracy, laminated tables can be developed for investigators to review when finalizing a report. The tables can provide a list of the approved locations, crime categories, date and time formats, and spelling of common terms. This technique provides for more accurate and complete data analysis, resulting in reduced crime.

Physical Security/Crime Prevention

In addition to the collection of incident demographic data, the investigative process should include ways to reduce the opportunity for future incidents to occur. In order to prevent future incidents, investigations and crime prevention should work together to provide recommendations that when implemented will stop future crimes. For many healthcare security departments, the investigation, crime prevention, and data analysis personnel are a small group of staff or just one person. Sometimes this one person is a supervisor or even the department director. However, the point is that the investigative process does not end with the investigation of an incident. It is the collection of data and the creation of solutions that when implemented will reduce the potential of future incidents.

When determining solutions for the reduction of future incidents, a team approach works best. After the investigation has been concluded, the investigation team, as discussed earlier in this chapter, should be brought together in order to develop and implement solutions that will reduce the potential for future incidents. When looking to determine solutions to reduce crime, a representative from the area in which the incident or incidents have occurred can be helpful in the recommendation process. This individual knows the area best and is well suited to determine what processes will be most effective in the reduction of crime.

Lost-and-Found Program

Patient and staff satisfaction are a major consideration for hospital administration. Establishing a lost-and-found program can provide a positive image for the security department and the hospital as a whole. Helping patients, visitors, and staff find missing or stolen property is good for the hospital's public relations and increases customer satisfaction. Many times, a patient will be admitted through the emergency department or transferred from a nursing home, and personal property like clothing and jewelry end up separated from the patient and lost. A security officer who presents to the patient and is interested in helping to find the property can provide very positive feelings for the patient who is dealing with more significant issues but is concerned or saddened by the loss of personal property. Many times, this property is in the hospital, left unmarked in the emergency department or left in a drawer at a nursing station. It is up to security to trace the steps of the patient, to interview staff, check the medical record, and search the patient's room or nursing station in order to look for the missing property.

The development of a lost-and-found program starts with the program definition. The security department should define its lost-and-found program: what property will be collected and investigated; how it will be returned to patients, visitors, and staff; where will it be stored; how long unclaimed property will be kept by the hospital; and how property will be disposed of.

The security department should decide what property it will collect as part of the lost-and-found program. Is it going to be patient property only, or will it include visitor and staff property, as well as hospital property? Will security have the staff to investigate all categories of lost-and-found property and follow up with all persons who lost property or spend time trying to find the owner of property found? When the owner of found property is determined, how will property be returned? Will property be mailed or delivered by security, or will owners have to come back to the hospital to pick up property. Storage will be an issue when a lost-and-found program is established. In healthcare, many times patient property is left behind on a nursing unit or in the emergency department. This property can build up depending on the time period for storage that is established by the lost-and-found policy. Clothing is the first property to be disposed of since it takes up the most space and has the least value. Hold it for 30 days from the time of receipt or 30 days after the investigation to determine the owner is closed. Personal items like cell phones, MP3 players, computers, or tablets should be held for 60 days—again, either after receipt or after the investigation is closed. Last is jewelry; jewelry should be held for 90 days or longer. Rings and other type of jewelry not only have a high monetary value but also have a high sentimental value. Returning lost jewelry has the highest impact on patients, visitors, and staff and their level of customer satisfaction.

Lastly, the lost-and-found program should determine how property will be disposed of. Before a program is established, determination should be made of how clothing, electronics, and jewelry will be disposed of after the holding time period has expired. Clothing should be destroyed. In most cases, clothing has no real value. Clothing determined to have a real high value should be given to charity. The same is true for cell phones, computers, or tablets. They should be given to charity. A charity should be selected before the lost-and-found program starts and arrangements should be made to ensure that these items will not be given to or sold to persons residing within the hospital's community of service so that property is not given to friends or associates of the person who lost the property. There are many charities that provide cell phones to battered women and the elderly. Also, many hospitals have their own charities. In that case, clothing can be given to the hospital charity for patients in need; however, electronics and jewelry should not be given to the hospital charity so that these items are not given to associates of the owner.

Jewelry is the most problematic property to dispose of. Many security departments will give it to their local police department to be destroyed.

Many police departments have established relationships with companies that will melt down the metal and resell the stones. This process ensures that the property will never be given to or sold to a person known by the owner. Some hospitals that do not have a police department that can assist will set up a relationship with a local pawn shop or sell the electronics or jewelry on eBay, with the proceeds going to hospital charities. This process should be avoided in order to keep the property from ending up in the hands of a friend or associate of the owner. In the case of jewelry, a relationship with a local jeweler can be set up to melt down the gold or silver and resell the stones. The last item to discuss is any contraband found within personal property, like knives, pills, and other substances. Knives and other sharps can be given to the local police department to be destroyed, like jewelry, or placed in a sharp's container. If a sharp's container is going to be used, the container company should be contacted to ensure that they can properly handle knives, etc. Pills should be given to the pharmacy to be destroyed with other expired medications. Remember, pills can no longer be thrown down the toilet per the Environmental Protection Agency (EPA). Other substances should be thrown out in the regular trash or in red bags to be incinerated. Again, the company that is disposing of the hospital's red bags should be contacted to ensure it is okay to throw security's discarded substances away. It is important to note that the disposal of any unknown substance should be conducted through a policy and procedure that is developed before the lost-and-found process starts. This policy should be created with the assistance of the hospital's legal department and, if deemed necessary, the local police department so that proper protocols will be followed.

Reference

1. Montgomery, Reginald J. and William J. Majeski. Parking Lot investigations. In *Corporate Investigations*. 2nd Ed. Tucson, AZ: Lawyers and Judges Publishing Company, 2005.

Chapter 6

Emergency Response

Introduction

By definition, a disaster or emergent event is considered any event that requires the use of more than the normal everyday amount of resources or personnel or potentially endangers the well-being of patients, visitors, or staff. In the healthcare setting, there are numerous events that could be considered emergent or disastrous. From a major event like a terrorist attack in the community to a smaller, more confined event like a chemical spill within the hospital, healthcare institutions must be prepared to manage a wide range of emergent events. Every hospital should be well prepared to respond to any emergent situation in a consistent and systematic manner. Healthcare institutions should have a plan that includes all levels of the organization, including hospital leaders and medical staff. Responsibilities should be periodically tested in the form of a drill or exercise to ensure that staff understand their role and can function effectively during an actual event. When any emergent event occurs, the hospital's emergency preparedness plan should be activated, and an emergency command center should be opened and staffed. Hospital staff, including security, should be well trained to handle any type of emergent situation and know their role and the response protocols. From a simple research laboratory refrigerator alarm to a community mass causality incident, security staff should be tested and always prepared to respond.

Preparing for an Emergent Event

The Federal Emergency Management Agency (FEMA) recommends that an emergency response address four phases: mitigation, preparedness, response, and recovery. FEMA defines each strategy and recommends that every disaster plan incorporate the four strategies within its response. The mitigation phase is designed to identify and reduce potential hazards and their impact before they occur. The emergency management plan should identify facility-specific prevention activities based on the priorities identified from local, state, or federal laws, such as fire codes, along with other mandates for accreditation agencies like the Joint Commission (TJC), Centers for Medicare & Medicaid Services (CMS), or National Fire Protection Association (NFPA). Utilizing the hospital's hazard vulnerability assessment (HVA) is important in the mitigation of potential emergency risks. Identifying risks and implementing strategies to reduce the risks is a major part of the emergency preparedness process. For example, mitigation strategies should include the redundancy of power, electrical, communications, and data management systems and backup procedures for the storage and retrieval of hospital supplies.

Preparedness activities focus on improving the response to and recovery from actual emergencies. The most important preparedness activity for a facility is the development of an emergency operations plan (EOP), which guides facility operations during an actual emergency. Properly training healthcare facility personnel, developing an incident management system (IMS), conducting drills and exercises, and regularly reviewing and improving the EOP are all important steps in the preparedness process.

Response activities are designed to control the negative effects of an emergent situation or incident, maximizing the capability to provide an emergency response and minimizing the impact of the hazard on the facility, staff, patients, and operations. While a healthcare facility's response begins after an incident has happened, personnel should be prepared to implement operations without prior notice. Response activities should unfold according to a preplanned progression, starting with the recognition that a disaster has occurred, reporting the disaster to key personnel, activating the EOP, and opening the command center. Notify all hospital personnel and mobilize them. Respond to the emergency and stay mobilized until the disaster is declared over. The goal of the recovery phase is to restore essential services and resume normal operations as quickly as possible. The recovery phase begins in tandem with the response phase, demobilizing staff and supplies once the disaster is over and starting the recovery process by going back to normal operations. Record all financial information pertaining to the disaster and the hospital's response.

In general, the more prepared an organization is to assume the recovery phase, the easier the transition will be back to normal operations. Many healthcare facilities underestimate the resources and time necessary to recover adequately from an emergency. Recovery operations should include provisions for staff, facility, and financial recovery. For many healthcare facilities, returning the facility to normal operations as quickly as possible is essential for financial survival. Plans should describe procedures for reestablishing normal operations following an emergency, including the person(s) who directs recovery operations and procedures for initiating recovery.[1]

Determining Preparedness Needs: The Hazard Vulnerability Assessment

The Joint Commission (TJC), along with the Centers for Medicare & Medicaid Services (CMS), requires all hospitals to have an emergency management plan for all of an institution's sites. This plan must describe in detail the organization's response to all types of emergencies within the hospital and the surrounding community. The first step in creating a plan is to conduct a hazard risk or vulnerability assessment for every hospital site. A hazard vulnerability assessment (HVA) identifies potential risks that could affect an organization's services, or its ability to provide those services. The HVA serves as a needs assessment for the emergency management program and includes the response to security-related incidents. The Joint Commission requires hospitals to conduct and annually review their HVA to meet regulatory standards. The HVA is designed to identify potential hazards and analyze what could happen if a hazard occurs. The HVA is used to prioritize specific and overall relative risks. The factors considered in the assessment include the assumption that the risk occurs at the worst possible time and with a full patient census. The most common HVA utilized by hospitals is the Kaiser Permanente tool. The Kaiser Foundation developed this tool to evaluate the risks associated with healthcare systems and processes and rank their probability of occurrence based on subjective factors outlined within the survey document. The evaluation of risk factors contributes to the overall score within the assessment and is comprises the risk of service disruption, the probability of occurrence, and the preparedness response when an event occurs. In evaluating the risk, the following factors should be considered:

- Threat to life and/or health
- The magnitude of service disruptions
- Potential damage from failure
- Financial impact and legal issues

The probability rating may be based on statistics and objective information or be intuitive and subjective. Factors to consider when evaluating probability include:

- Known risk
- Historical data
- Manufacturer or vendor data

The hospital's ability to manage the risk is based on preparedness, the ability to manage an event when it occurs. Items to be considered include:

- Status of current plans
- Training
- Insurance
- Backup systems
- Community resources

In the evaluation or assessment of hazards, the ones that can cause significant injuries to patients, visitors, and staff should be prioritized as the highest risk. The potential for environmental impact should be considered second, followed by consideration of the impact on the surrounding community and other stakeholders.

Incident Command System

The National Incident Management System (NIMS) is a systematic management approach to guide hospitals and government agencies to work together to manage incidents involving all threats and hazards, regardless of cause, size, location, or complexity. NIMS provides a flexible but standardized set of incident management practices, with emphasis on common principles. By using NIMS, hospitals become part of a comprehensive national approach to disaster response that creates an incident command system (ICS).[2] TJC and CMS advise healthcare organizations to take an "all-hazards" approach to emergency management, an approach that focuses on capacities and capabilities critical to preparedness for a full spectrum of emergencies or disasters. TJC recommends using NIMS to manage disaster situations. An all-hazards approach focuses on flexibility and scalability to adapt to a wide variety of disasters, focusing on the continuity of essential services that must remain consistent regardless of the type of disaster. Utilizing a hazard vulnerability analysis helps facilities assess risk by examining the likelihood of particular events and evaluating the extent to which they will impair a facility's operations and essential services.[3]

An all-hazards approach creates a plan and structure that is flexible enough to scale to any emergency as it occurs and evolves. A single hazard may evolve to include aspects of another hazard. For example, a utility failure may lead to the need for an evacuation. An all-hazards command structure includes:

- Flexible structure for response to a variety of emergencies
- Clear delineation of staff roles and responsibilities
- Predictable chain of command
- Accountability for staff involved
- Prioritized response checklists
- Use of common terminology to reduce miscommunication
- Ability to be integrated into a community-wide plan[4]

Emergency Operations Plan

The EOP provides the structure and processes that the organization utilizes to respond to and initially recover from an event. The EOP needs to include the identification of specific procedures to mitigate, prepare for, respond to, and recover from an emergent situation. The disaster plan needs to demonstrate proper planning and response, which includes:

1. Identifying a leader to oversee emergency management preparation and response.
2. Having and staffing a command center that uses a common command structure (NIMS) that links with the command structure of the community.

3. Having a communication system that works both internally and externally with community partners: state, federal, and local emergency and law enforcement agencies. Provide backup in the event of system failures during emergencies.

4. Developing a formal cooperation among healthcare organizations within the community that together provide services to a contiguous geographic area (for example, among hospitals serving a town or borough) and have the ability to meet the clinical needs of patients.

5. Ensuring that the hospital has adequate supplies and utilities to maintain services for the entire length of the event, up to 96 hours, or provide an alternative means for providing essential building utilities and services.

6. Being able to maintain hospital operations and protect all patients, staff, and property.

7. Maintaining care and support for vulnerable populations, like infants, behavioral health patients, and the elderly.

8. Periodically testing the emergency plan by evaluating the plan's appropriateness, adequacy, and effectiveness. Testing or exercising should stress the capabilities and performance of the plan using real-life scenarios that are relevant to the organization and based on the hospital's HVA.

9. Providing tests or exercises at least twice a year, in response to either an actual emergency or a planned exercise. At least one exercise needs to include an influx of actual or simulated patients. At least one exercise each year should include the community and be part of a community-wide response. For all drills or exercises, security should be involved in the planning process and participate in the drill.[5]

Other considerations in creating an emergency preparedness plan include:

■ Staff and staff family support: Housing, transportation, incident stress debriefing
■ Communication with the media
■ Provisions for the evacuation of the entire facility (both horizontally and vertically) when the environment cannot support adequate patient care and treatment
■ Facilities for the decontamination of radioactive, biological, and chemical agents

- Alternate roles and responsibilities of personnel during emergencies, including who they report to within the organization's command structure
- Procedures for an annual evaluation of the organization's hazard vulnerability analysis and of the emergency management plan, including its objectives, scope, functionality, and effectiveness

General Security Procedures in Disaster Response

Hospital security staff need to be prepared in the event of an emergent event. There is a general assumption that hospitals will be notified of an emergent situation. It's important to recognize that not all emergencies are reported beforehand; many times security staff will come in contact with an emergent situation without prior or proper notification. To effectively manage disasters, security officers need to learn to identify the type of disaster, notify senior management and hospital personnel, and properly react to any emergent situation. For the security department, basic protocols should be put in place for every disaster situation and continuous training should be conducted so that staff retain information pertinent to disaster response.

Incident Notification

Incident notification is the most important sequence of events in the management of a disaster. In general, the security department coordinates disaster notification or responds to calls related to emergent events. To effectively manage an emergent incident, security must be notified immediately of a pending disaster. If an incident is suspected, security should be ready to immediately activate the disaster plan.

Once an emergent event is identified, security must notify key personnel of the event. When the event is small, like a refrigerator alarm or a chemical spill, notification may be to only one or two key personnel. If the incident is larger, requiring a large section or all of the hospital to respond, then the notification scheme is more complicated. Today, electronic mass notification systems are used to notify staff and/or patients/visitors of a disaster situation. If an electronic solution is not available, then a notification tree should be developed and implemented. A notification or call tree is a list of priority persons to call when an emergency occurs. The idea behind a call tree is to provide notification to a small number of staff who will in turn call other staff, who will again call even more staff. In most cases, call trees reflect the hospital's organizational structure. Security would call senor staff, who in turn would call their department heads or managers. The tree should be designed so that the number of calls is limited, allowing staff to respond to the disaster quickly rather than spending time on the phone calling staff or answering questions. In either case, the message should be short and concise, so response is quick. Messages should state the type of disaster, the location, the time it occurred, and a condensed response protocol, if needed.

Initial Response by Security

The priority for security is to secure the incident location and ensure proper traffic control, providing free and unobstructed access for emergency vehicles into the emergency department. It is important to continually maintain a clear roadway throughout hospital property, especially into and out of the emergency department. Pedestrian traffic flow needs to be controlled as well. Entrances may need to be closed and persons wishing to enter the hospital may need to be questioned prior to entering to determine their needs. If the event is occurring within the hospital, it is important that security or the persons working within the affected area secure the area so that only essential personnel have access. Nonessential hospital personnel, patients, and visitors should be removed and restricted from the area. For both traffic and access control, nonsecurity personnel may be needed to assist security if staffing levels cannot support both functions. Written within the EOP should be procedures for nonsecurity personnel to assist security. These procedures should be implemented immediately upon the declaration of a disaster situation.

Identification of Exposure

Security officers need to be trained on the different types of exposures— chemical, radiological, biological, and pandemic—so they can identify potential victims before they are permitted access into the hospital. Many times, when an external event occurs, hospital notification may be delayed, and victims could arrive at the hospital before the hospital is prepared.

Victims may intuitively go to their local hospital for treatment, not understanding the potential risks they may create. Security staff need to learn to identify the symptoms of exposure for the most common biological and chemical agents, symptoms of exposure to a radiological source, and flu symptoms. Training should be ongoing and continuous so that staff remember symptom types and response procedures. When a mass causality incident occurs involving a biological, chemical, or radiological substance or there is a large-scale flu epidemic, security personnel need to step outside of hospital entrances in order to screen persons before they enter. This is important so that victims do not contaminate the hospital and its treatment areas or expose others to the pathogen.

Lockdown Procedures

It is important that all hospitals have an appropriate "lockdown procedure" in the event of a mass casualty or internal incident. In the event of an incident involving exposure, hospital security personnel must know what procedures to follow in a quick and efficient manner. Security staff must be an integral part of the exposure notification process; they must know whether to institute a partial or full facility lockdown. During a disaster situation, security officers posted at access portals should step outside of the hospital buildings to physically stop persons and screen them as potential victims. The hospital disaster plan should include procedures for the identification of access portals for hospital staff, disaster victims, disaster victim family members, the media, delivery personnel, and regular inpatient visitors. Each of the above categories should be segregated and a procedure established to provide entry and cueing guidelines.

Full Facility Lockdown

In the event of a major incident, an external mass causality incident, or mass destruction of hospital property, the hospital may need to lock down the entire facility, except for emergency operations. This is done for the protection of the hospital from contamination or restricting access to internal affected areas. During a major incident, the hospital may receive a large number of victims or a number of victims that are contaminated. It is important for the hospital to control and screen traffic, both vehicular and pedestrian. In the development of the EOP, security must be prepared to close entrances and funnel staff, potential victims, press, and family members into specific entrances and areas of the hospital. Written within the EOP should be a designated area for the media that is separated from the treatment areas, and a place for family to meet that is separate from the media and treatment areas. Potential victims need to be funneled to specific areas for evaluation and treatment.

The remaining entrances and exits during a full lockdown may need to be locked so that entry and/or exit are restricted. This may not always be possible, so entrances and exits may have to be staffed with security officers or other hospital staff assigned to the security function. Either way, conducting a full facility or even a partial facility lockdown requires planning and drilling to ensure that staff understand the process and their duties at each location. Planning includes the prior evaluation of each entry and exit portal to see if they can be locked physically and meet the fire code and determining what impact locking a door will have during a disaster situation.

Partial Facility Lockdown

The security department should prepare to implement a partial facility lockdown when necessary. Depending on the type and extent of the disaster, a partial facility lockdown may be in order. If details are incomplete as to the magnitude of an event, the hospital may wish to only implement a partial lockdown until more information is available as to the extent of the disaster. Oftentimes, this entails the closing of certain entrances or areas of the hospital in order to funnel the media and family members to specific areas, as well as directing potential victims to treatment areas. As an example, a hospital may want to curtail access to all clinic areas or business offices so that it is better able to redeploy staff to the emergency treatment areas.

Emergency Department Lockdown

At some point during a disaster, it may be necessary to lock down the emergency department (ED). The locking down of the ED may occur because of contamination or the need to restrict access into the area by unauthorized staff, visitors, or patients. If the ED becomes contaminated, security may be required to keep all patients and staff inside of the area and restrict outsiders from entering until the area can be decontaminated. That requires the posting of security at every entrance and exit of the emergency department. Many hospitals utilize electronic access control for this purpose, locking all doors only and allowing access by the stationed security officer or a limited number of persons with card access privileges.

Decontamination/Treatment Process

All security officers need to become familiar with the decontamination and treatment processes associated with contamination or pandemic flu victim incidences. Officers should participate in decontamination training and be part of the decontamination process, so that they can properly direct potential victims to assigned treatment areas. Victims must be isolated from hospital staff to avoid facility-wide contamination. With respect to mass casualty incidents, victims may be required to disrobe and undergo scrub-down to remove contaminates prior to being treated. Pandemic flu victims may not require decontamination; however, they will require isolation and segregation in order to not infect hospital staff.

Biological Agents

Anthrax (*Bacillus anthracis*) is an acute infection of the skin, lungs, or gastrointestinal system. Its related spores can survive for a few days in temperatures as high as 318°F and can remain viable in soil and water for years or even decades. About 8,000 to 10,000 spores are required to cause pulmonary infection and 1,000 spores for intestinal infection. If diagnosed quickly, anthrax is treatable with several different types of antibiotics. Skin contact creates sores or blisters that can develop into an infection. Inhalation or ingestion of bacterial spores causes one to develop flu-like symptoms within one to seven days of exposure. After two to four days, victims have difficulty breathing, often experience severe exhaustion, and may develop a fever. There is a 90% fatality rate for untreated inhalation.

Ebola is a virus that requires direct contact with the blood or secretions of bodily fluids. It is the most dangerous virus known to science. It causes death in 50%–90% of all exposure cases. The virus is in incubation for 2–21 days. Symptoms include fever, weakness, muscle pain, headache, and sore throat, often associated with vomiting, rash, diarrhea, and internal and external bleeding.

Smallpox, the variola virus, is an infection that occurs from contact with blood or secretions of bodily fluids, or via inhalation from infected persons. The incubation period is about 12 days. Symptoms include malaise, fever, vomiting, and headaches. Victims develop a rash, which blisters within two to three days. Smallpox is generally not fatal, but a victim must be in isolation for 16–17 days from the onset of the virus.

Ricin is a toxin made from the leftover mash of the castor bean, which is processed for the production of castor oil. It is easily accessible and is easy to produce. It can be inhaled or ingested. It kills body cells on contact. Death occurs within 36–48 hours after exposure. There is no cure for this toxin. A large aerosol dose is required to be effective, at least 320 mg.

Hazardous Chemical Agents

Cyanide is a common chemical agent used in ore extraction, tanning, and electroplating. Cyanide in a liquid form emits a heavy gas that smells like bitter almonds. It poisons victims through inhalation of gas. Inhalation of cyanide blocks the ability of the body's cells to consume oxygen, which causes the cells to die. Exposure causes irritation to the eyes, nausea, dizziness, weakness, and anxiety. This is followed by convulsions, unconsciousness, and then death. The longer the exposure to or the higher the concentration of cyanide, the quicker a victim will be contaminated and die.

Mustard gas is a blistering agent; it is an oily liquid that is heavier than water. The vapors and/or liquid are the danger. The liquid and gas have the odor of mustard, onions, or garlic. Two to 24 hours after exposure a victim will notice eye irritation, burning of the skin, and upper airway irritation. High concentrations of exposure will cause blistering of the skin, eyes, and throat. Then it is absorbed into the body, where it damages cells and causes death.

Sarin gas is a nerve gas. It disrupts the mechanism by which nerves communicate with the organs, causing overstimulation of the organs. Sarin is a clear, colorless liquid that emits a heavy gas that sinks to the ground. The gas is odorless. Exposure causes a diminishment of the pupils, runny nose, and shortness of breath. Large exposures can cause loss of consciousness, convulsions, and death.

Radiation Exposure

Radiation poisoning is caused by exposure to irradiated uranium that gives off alpha and gamma rays. Exposure can be caused by exploding a nuclear device, which gives off massive amounts of these rays, or via the exploding of an irradiated source that distributes thousands of finite pieces throughout the explosion area. Exposure to radiation causes body cell disruption or death. The cell disruption affects the bloodstream and gastrointestinal areas. Symptoms often include nausea, vomiting, and malaise, followed by a symptom-free period. Major organ malfunction occurs from cell death, causing body functions to shut down and subsequent death. For mild cases of exposure, a victim can take iodine, which will absorb the radiation and help the body to pass the radiation out of the body.

Pandemic Flu

All forms of flu present an identification challenge to the healthcare security officer. The difference between a pandemic flu victim and a person with a bad cold may be minute. To protect a hospital from being contaminated by pandemic flu, early intervention is important. Notification of the potential of a pandemic event is all that is necessary for a hospital to go on alert and commence the screening of all persons entering the facility. With respect to this form of flu, security operatives must protect themselves from airborne contamination. To prevent contamination, operatives should slip into water-resistant attire, don a M-95 respirator device, and wear protective goggles while screening persons.

In the event of a pandemic flu outbreak, the hospital may be required to close their doors to all persons except the sick and working staff. In the event of such an incident, security officers should be assigned to each access portal to screen all incoming individuals. Similar to other exposures, once a victim is classified as being at "risk," it's imperative that they be dispatched to the emergency room via walking outside of the hospital and entering in a designated area. The most difficult part of disaster response in a pandemic flu event is identifying flu victims. Although there is no quick, sure-fire method of diagnosing a pandemic flu from the common cold or other illness, one efficient method of assessment is through body temperature. The most effective way to determine that an individual has a fever, on a mass scale, is through the use of an infrared thermal imaging device.

These instruments are similar to the devices used by electricians to locate "hot spots" in wiring schematics; the device is pointed at a person and accurately determines an individual's body temperature. A high body temperature potentially means the individual has the flu.

Personal Protection Equipment

Security officers must learn to use personal protective equipment (PPE) when disaster strikes. PPE is necessary to wear in order to protect officers from exposure to any dangerous substances. Different PPE is utilized depending on the type of potential exposure. Practicing the donning of different PPE costumes is important in the preparation drills normally associated with mass causality incidents. It is recommended that security staff utilize either Level D or Level C decontamination equipment.

Level D protection—Consists of work clothes or, in the case of security, the security uniform. The Level D uniform consists of a light fluid-resistant gown, latex gloves, goggles for eye protection, and an M-95 respirator face mask. Level D protection is utilized for biological and flu situations and is worn by security officers at access portals, in treatment areas, or when guarding patients.

Level C protection—Consists of a "Tyvek" plastic full-body suit with a hood embodying a full-face M-40 respirator, rubber boots or work boots, and heavy rubber gloves. A security officer should wear this level of protection when confronted with chemical and radiological exposures.[5]

References

1. Lessons Learned Information Sharing. Best practice, emergency management programs for healthcare facilities: The four phases of emergency management. 2017. www.LLIS.com.
2. California Emergency Preparedness. Preparing Hospitals for Disasters. 2018. *Hazards Vulnerability Analysis: Revised HVA Tool for Kaiser Permanente.* https://www.calhospitalprepare.org/hazard-vulnerability-analysis.

3. FEMA. *NIMS Doctrine Supporting Guides & Tools.* https://www.fema.gov/nims-doctrine-supporting-guides-tools.
4. Weden, Mary Lou. Defining an "All Hazards" approach to hospital emergency management. Intermedix, September 9, 2016. http://preparedness.intermedix.com/blog/defining-an-all-hazards-approach-to-hospital-emergency-management.
5. Scaglione, Bernard J. and Anthony J. Luizzo. Training security officers to recognize the perils of weapons of mass destruction and Pandemic Flu contaminates. *Journal of Healthcare Protection Management*, Vol. 23, No. 2, 2007, 1–9.

Chapter 7

Customer Satisfaction: Enhancing the Patient Experience

Introduction

Security and customer service are synonymous in healthcare. For decades, hospitals have tracked security and safety satisfaction as part of their overall patient satisfaction process. Many hospitals feel strongly about their security department providing customer service since a security officer is usually the first person a patient or visitor interacts with when they enter the hospital. Many believe that the security officer stationed in the main lobby or in the emergency department waiting area has a direct influence on the overall satisfaction of patients, visitors, and staff who utilize the hospital's services.

Many hospitals dedicate large amounts of resources and funding for customer service training. For security, they focus on uniforms, personal appearance, greetings, and surveys in order to improve customer service scores. They outfit security officers in blazers and ties or polo shirts instead of standard military uniforms in order to create a more welcoming environment. They script officers so that greetings and messages are the same and pay third-party survey companies hundreds of thousands of dollars to determine satisfaction levels.

Hospital Consumer Assessment of Healthcare Providers and Systems

The healthcare customer service arena is changing. Recently, the Centers for Medicare & Medicaid Services (CMS) implemented a survey tool in order to establish a national benchmark for patient satisfaction. Called the Hospital Consumer Assessment of Healthcare Providers and Systems (HCAHPS) survey, all hospitals that accept Medicare and Medicaid funding are required to participate in it. CMS started publishing the results of patient satisfaction scores through HCAHPS on its Hospital Compare website in 2008. As of October 2012, HCAHPS has been utilized to financially reward healthcare institutions that achieve higher than national average patient satisfaction survey scores. In order to accomplish this, in 2012 CMS started to withhold 1% of its payments to hospitals in order to create a pool of bonuses. During the first year of implementation, CMS withheld close to $850 million in Medicare and Medicaid payments to hospitals. As of 2013, patient satisfaction scores determined 30% of hospital's Medicare and Medicaid payment bonuses, while clinical measures for basic quality care determined the other 70%. CMS estimates that more than 3,000 hospitals are affected by this reimbursement change.

The HCAHPS survey was designed to reflect patients' perspectives on several key aspects of hospital service:

- Communication with doctors and nurses
- Responsiveness of hospital staff
- Pain management
- Communication about medicines
- Discharge information
- Cleanliness of the hospital environment
- Quietness of the hospital environment
- Overall satisfaction of hospital services

Healthcare security is not directly mentioned in the HCAHPS process. There are no security questions within the HCAHPS survey; however, two questions are seen by many hospital administrators as influenced by security. These regard the quietness of the hospital environment and the overall satisfaction with hospital services. The survey asks, "Using any number from 0 to 10, where 0 is the worst hospital possible and 10 is the best hospital possible, what number would you use to rate this hospital during your stay?"

and "Would you recommend this hospital to your friends and family?" For noise levels, the question reads: "During this hospital stay, how often was the area around your room quiet at night?" The survey provides four answer options to this question: never, sometimes, usually, and always.

The questions that ask the survey takers to rate the hospital stay and if they would recommend the hospital to others are both indicators of the overall hospital satisfaction. No matter who the patient encounters during their hospital stay, that employee may influence the patient's overall satisfaction and rating level. That is why many hospital administrators believe that security at the main entrance to the hospital, in the emergency room waiting area, patrolling the hospital, or responding to take a report may be a contributor to the overall patient satisfaction score. Security may influence the score during visiting hours when screening visitors and administering passes, when security comes to collects patient valuables, or even when a security officer approaches a patient or visitor that seems lost. The survey also evaluates the level of noise within the hospital. Many hospitals use overhead paging systems and nurse call systems that are heard throughout inpatient rooms and clinic treatment areas. Many hospital administrators believe that this noise, along with open-mike walkie-talkie calls from security, facilities, housekeeping, and patient transport, contributes to the noise level outside patient rooms and treatment areas. Many hospitals now prohibit overhead paging and open speakers for walkie-talkies. This requires security personnel to use earpieces connected to their walkie-talkies. These measures dramatically reduce the level of noise in clinical areas, especially when security officers are on patrol or responding to calls within inpatient units after hours.[1]

Customer Service Research and Ideology

Current research and ideology on customer service thinking is changing the way customer satisfaction is viewed and how several organizations administer their program. The basic philosophies that drove customer service ideology in the past are being replaced as more research is being conducted. New research focuses on customer loyalty as opposed to satisfaction, determining that patient loyalty is more important than satisfaction because loyal patients are more likely to continue to use the services of hospitals that meet their particular needs.

In healthcare, patient satisfaction is sometimes focused on beautification and cleanliness. Many hospitals spend hundreds of thousands of dollars or even millions of dollars improving the look of the hospital, making sure that the hospital is clean and looks like a five-star hotel. For security, hospitals spend hundreds of dollars on security uniforms and focus on security officer appearance. Although important, studies show that this has no relationship with patient satisfaction or loyalty. However, studies do show that appearance and cleanliness are directly related to reducing the anxiety and negative stigma associated with hospitals and clinical care. J.D. Power and Associates conducted a survey on health-care customer service entitled "2012 National Patient Experience Study." According to the study, high patient satisfaction was not a fancy hospital lobby or high-tech equipment; it was staff. When the firm looked at the inpatient and outpatient hospital experience, it found that "patient satisfaction was most influenced by human factors." As a result, J.D. Power suggests that it is more worthwhile to invest in finding and keeping staff with superior interpersonal skills than constructing fancy renovations of lobbies and public spaces.[2]

Research completed at Brigham and Women's Hospital, published in the March 2013 edition of the *Journal of Postdoctoral Research.*, entitled "Patient Experience and Patient-Centered Care—Do We Really Care?" interviewed more than 1,000 physicians and nurses at four academic hospitals in Denmark, Israel, the United Kingdom, and the United States. The study found that only 1 in 10 clinicians stated that their department had a structured plan to improve the patient experience. Only one-third of the interviewees recalled receiving feedback from hospital management regarding patient satisfaction, and only 38% remembered actions conducted to improve it. Overall, many of those surveyed believed that achieving a high level of patient satisfaction was important for clinical success and could be achieved by:

- Better communication with patients
- Being attentive and responsive to patients' concerns and needs
- Being involved in the patient's clinical decision-making process[3]

A University of Albany study on patient satisfaction in the emergency department concluded that patient satisfaction was strongly correlated to a physician's interpersonal skills and was not correlated to diagnostic and therapeutic treatment expectations. Satisfaction was directly related to how patients were treated on a personal level. Surveyed patients reported being "very satisfied" when they received:

- An explanation for time spent in the emergency department
- An explanation of their medical condition
- Time with their physician

This study concluded that investing in interpersonal and communication skills was a practical way to improve patient satisfaction within the emergency department.[4]

In 2009, a 13-hospital system in the Midwest was used in a study to find out what influences patients to rate their overall hospital experience as "excellent." The study indicated that only patients who mark "excellent" are loyal patients and continued to use that hospital's services. Research was conducted by utilizing a telephone-based survey of discharged patients. For each hospital, a random sample of patients was contacted 7–14 days after discharge, and again at final medical disposition. The results of the study found that the attribute that influenced an "excellent" rating was staff care. This was followed by nursing care, physician care, the admission process, and room and food, in that order. In the study, staff care was defined as:

- Staff's willingness to help when patients had a question or concern
- Responsiveness of the staff to patient's requests
- Courtesy and helpfulness of the staff
- Amount of dignity and respect shown by the staff
- Clear and complete explanation provided by the staff about medications and their side effects
- Clear and complete explanation provided by the staff about home care

The study concluded that for healthcare organizations to obtain higher patient satisfaction scores, healthcare managers need to engage staff in courtesy, response, and basic communication skills in order to obtain an "excellence" rating.[5]

As outlined in "Patient Satisfaction: The Hospitalist's Role" by Dr. Patrick J. Torcson, a useful definition of the clinician's role in patient satisfaction is that of caring and concern demonstrated by:

- Attentiveness
- Dignity and respect
- Effective information transfer
- Shared decision making

The study determined attentiveness as a means of establishing a person-to-person connection with the patient, talking to them as individuals, not just as another patient. Attentiveness is demonstrated by showing curiosity about the patient as a person, using open-ended questions to gather clinical data, orienting patients, and continually communicating the process of care. Demonstrate dignity and respect through the performance of empathy. Often confused with sympathy, empathy is the understanding of a patient's feelings. Being empathetic means sitting down with the patient, explaining processes in plain language, maintaining eye contact, and using appropriate touches and nonverbal communication. Be aware of their nonverbal actions, such as demeanor, body posture, and verbal tone. Use a patient's own words and outwardly address a patient's feelings. The study concluded that clinicians need to provide information that:

- Addresses the cognitive, behavioral, and affective needs of patients and their families
- Is mindful of language discrepancies, time constraints, and the ability of patients to remember as barriers to effective communication
- Considers that patients want to share in the decision-making process regarding their care
- Discusses all-important decisions and presents patients and families with treatment options and then solicits their preferences[6]

According to research conducted by the Technical Assistance Research Program (TARP) on customer satisfaction, customers reward companies that do the basics well, proactively keep their customer informed, and are well educated, offering the right products and providing consistently good service. This behavior actually creates delight and significantly raises the level of customer loyalty. TARP's research also found that personal service interactions have 20 times the positive impact in fostering word-of-mouth referrals, and friendly 90-second interactions create an emotional connection that positively cements the relationship with the customer.[7]

Fred Lee, the author of *If Disney Ran Your Hospital: 9½ Things You Would Do Differently*, suggests that satisfaction does not equate to patient loyalty or continued use of services. It is loyalty that determines repeat customer business. Loyalty is generated by memorable events that happen when least expected. Patients reserve their good word of mouth and loyalty for hospitals where they feel their needs were anticipated and met by courteous, caring staff. However, Lee reminds us that patients judge loyalty by their own perceptions, sometimes subjective and not always translating the same way for everyone. Lee describes several factors that Disney, Press Ganey, and Gallop have found convert patient satisfaction into loyalty.

- Focusing on team responsibility, which means working together to solve problems and meet patient demands.
- Improving staff competence and skills by training staff on how to do their job and increasing their competence by continually educating them on changing processes and policies.
- Ensuring that staff are doing their job correctly and consistently and seeking measurable results to determine how well they are doing.
- Eliminating carelessness and creating an environment of consistent service. Have no tolerance for rudeness and never miss an opportunity for courtesy or compassion.

Fred Lee explains that the single most important need for a patient is for assurance, and he defines assurance as confidence of mind or manner; easy freedom from self-doubt or uncertainty; something that inspires or tends to inspire confidence. Lee cites Florence Nightingale, who wrote in her *Notes on Nursing* in 1846, "Apprehension, uncertainty, waiting and fear of surprise, do a patient more harm than any exertion…. Always tell a patient, and tell him beforehand, when you are going out and when you will be back, whether it is for a day, an hour or ten minutes."[8]

In a study on community police titled "Policing for People," Stephen D. Mastrofski defined "community policing" as a means to reduce crime and disorder, calm fears about threats to public safety, and reduce the public's alienation from social institutions like the police. In his study, he emphasized the importance of police service as a way to enhance community policing. He defined "good service" as being attentive because people want their service providers to pay attention to them. For the police, this means putting more officers on the street, increasing the ability for the police to be present, and hence more attention. Mastrofski defines "attentiveness" as the amount of time officers spend with people; the more time on the streets, the more attention that can be committed to people and resolving their problems. Additionally, traumatized victims—the injured, ill, assaulted, emotionally upset, and mentally ill—require more attention, comfort, and reassurance from the police. The second element to policing is reliability. People expect police to be responsive, providing service that is timely and error-free. Even a good-faith effort by a police officer is often appreciated as much as a favorable outcome. Studies show that people are pleased, often surprised, when police complete a job or check to see how things worked out. Police must be responsive even when they deny a citizen's request. The public wants competent police officers who get the job done, officers who know how to deal with difficult situations.

Mastrofski believes that police officers need to have proper manners. The public judges police competence primarily in terms of tangible things like proper manners. Studies show that bad manners are among the most frequent complaints against the police. The most powerful predictors of citizen satisfaction with the police have more to do with how police treated them than with completion of their call. A number of studies show that citizens are more likely to obey the law and less likely to be disorderly or violent when police enforce the law in a manner that is respectful. The final element of policing according to Mastrofski is fairness.[9] Tom Tyler (1990) found that people who perceived that legal officials, like the police, treated them fairly had a stronger inclination to obey the law in the future. Tyler found that the most important element of procedural fairness was people's trust in the authorities' motives, treating citizens with dignity and respect, having a sense of decision-maker neutrality, and providing citizens with an opportunity to participate in the decision.[10]

Creating a Customer Service Program

The research presented in this chapter is not specific to security and in a few cases not even related to healthcare at all; however, the studies presented above all come to the same conclusions. No matter the industry, the themes to great customer service are the same. It is not the physical environment that creates loyal customers; it is the people and their interaction that influences satisfaction and loyalty the most. When creating a customer service program in healthcare, the focus of the program should always be the patients, visitors, and staff perception of security: their feelings of security while residing within the hospital. A solid customer service program needs to combine basic security concepts with customer service skills. When basic customer service principles are combined with basic principles of security, a high level of security service can be obtained while enhancing customer service.

An effective customer service program begins with looking at the patient and visitor experience within the hospital through the eyes of the patients and visitors. This process starts with a physical walk-through of the patient and visitor process from entry onto hospital property to discharge and exit. Start from parking the car, being dropped off by car or taxi, or entry by ambulance. The process should continue through admission, preadmission testing, and then on to treatment and inpatient and outpatient locations, ending with the discharge process. Spend time observing the security procedures at all these locations, looking specifically at what security measures are in place or need to be implemented. Note their visibility to patients, visitors, and staff and determine what obstacles prevent patients and visitors from having a positive security experience. Interview staff, patients, and visitors at key points of the security experience to learn the patient/ visitor process and their experience in navigating through security in the hospital. Areas should be identified that create barriers to customer service: doors that stick, don't lock, have broken latches, or are hard to pull open. Processes and procedures should be permanently fixed so that access into the hospital is less stressful, but secure. Are security officers knowledgeable enough to direct patients and visitors to every department, clinic, or doctor's office within and outside of the hospital? When a person enters the emergency department (ED), does the security officer greet them appropriately and provide detailed information on the ED admission and treatment process to reduce patient anxiety and fear? For example, access into a hospital during the day was obtained at each level of the three-story parking garage. However, at night the doors on the second and third floors were locked. Visitors walked from the parking lot through an initial set of doors only to pull on a set of fire doors further down the corridor that were locked. The doors on the second and third floors were locked to restrict access to only the first floor, where visitors could be screened. However, there was no signage on the second and third floor doors indicating they were locked during the off hours, only a card reader for staff to access. If someone was leaving the hospital and the fire doors were open, unauthorized persons could access the hospital without being screened. When the doors were locked, visitors had to enter a stairwell that brought them to the ground floor, where they could access the hospital; however, there was no signage to explain that process. If you were handicapped in any way, you had no choice but to exit the hospital back into the parking lot to get into your car and drive to the first level in order to gain entry. Because of poor signage and no surveillance to monitor these areas by security off hours, access was frustrating to visitors and patients and created a lot of anger toward security. The solution was to place signage at the garage entrance at night and at the first set of doors on the second and third floors, stating the door access hours. Also, CCTV and an intercom were placed at second and third floor entry points so that security could monitor and talk to visitors and visitors could talk to security.

As part of the walk-through, it is important to consider the mental condition of patients and visitors as well as physical conditions when utilizing the hospital. Patients' and visitors' minds are preoccupied with the status of their own health or the health of a loved one. They are worried about living or dying, whether they need to make funeral arrangements, or simply how they will pay the bills while they or their spouse is not working. In general, patients and visitors do not pay attention to the hospital environment; they are scared, afraid of the hospital and their treatment or the treatment to their loved one. These considerations should be kept in mind while assessing patient and visitor navigation through the hospital's physical environment and determining security services.

Integrating Security into the Customer Service Process

In order for security to be effective while providing a customer-friendly environment, there needs to be a consistent security presence throughout the organization. This includes the off-site facilities as well as the main campus. Security presence means a visible CCTV camera or security officer, but more importantly, the perception by patients, visitors, and staff that there is a security program in place. It is important that everyone entering or present within the hospital feel secure. For example, many times the security officer posted in the main lobby is positioned off to the side of the entrance or deep into the lobby, lost among other services or sitting in a chair behind a desk leaning back reading a book or newspaper. Security officers should be present at all entrances, positioned to greet persons entering and assist them if necessary. Additionally, many organizations do not completely commit to a visitor pass system, creating an inconsistent system with many ways to circumvent the process. If a visitor pass or visitor check process is implemented, it should be implemented consistently, and security should be provided with the proper resources to implement it correctly. The physical presence of a security program that is felt by patients, visitors, and staff helps reduce crime. Security must be visible, look professional, and be consistently posted or patrolling in the hospital. Patients, visitors, and staff should see security in every place, whether being treated, visiting, or at work. This means seeing a uniformed security officer in the lobby all of the time or consistently patrolling the interior and exterior of the hospital. Ensure that CCTV camera domes are visible to patients, visitors, and staff. Ensure that doors designated to be locked are locked. Consistently screen persons at entrances, issue visitor passes to everyone, and ensure that all areas of the campus are well lit at night. The visible presence of security officers, CCTV, and access control systems helps to deter crime and increases the feeling of security within the hospital. Lastly, there needs to be a security response. This does not just mean the security officer rushing to the scene of an emergency, but the immediate repair of a broken lock or electronic security equipment, and the quick replacement of burned-out lights in parking areas, stairwells, and other isolated areas. People, in general, are very perceptive and notice and feel the lack of security—from the parking garage light that has been burned out for the past six months or the staff entry door where the lock has been broken for the past few months. The need to immediately repair broken security devices is just as important to the patient, visitor, and staff as the quick response of security officers to a security emergency. Security presence, visibility, and response are important to providing a quality security program in which patients, visitors, and staff can feel and see the presence of security. The feeling of security when staying, visiting, and working is essential to the customer service process.

Staff Training

Studies conclude that investing in interpersonal and communication skills is the most practical way to improve patient satisfaction. As previously stated, customer service is about human factors demonstrating attributes that provide a caring but affirmative environment, exhibiting attributes like:

■ Attentiveness
■ Dignity/respect
■ Communication
■ Courtesy/manners
■ Responsiveness
■ Scripting
■ Consistent service

These attributes drive customer loyalty and need to be integrated into the security customer service program. From security management all the way down to the security officer, commitment and training of the human factor must be present within the security department to provide for a high level of customer service.

Customer service education should start with the creation of a program that outlines the goals of the officers while posted and on patrol, and demonstrates their specific duties related to customer service. This training should be conducted annually. Security staff need to be knowledgeable about the hospital, specific clinical departments, policies and procedures, and of course, treatment processes. As stated in the research, patients and visitors do not always ask the questions on their mind, so the training program should include security officer education on a message that would answer the most basic questions that would be asked by a patient or visitor. The program should also consider the physical condition of patients, visitors, or even staff. Sometimes hospitals forget that they are servicing the sick, those that require wheelchairs, crutches, and canes; have difficulty walking long distances; are in need of a place to stop and sit during their walk to a specific department, clinic, or doctor's office; or have difficulty verbally communicating or reading.

Attentiveness

Security officers should be attentive while on duty. Attentiveness means being engaged, showing the willingness to assist, and establishing a connection with the patient, visitor, or staff member. This process starts with first contact: a friendly hello or good morning, presenting a positive first impression and minimizing obstacles to the perception of attentiveness. This includes providing one-to-one communication during greetings and all interactions, paying attention to persons as they enter the hospital and to persons that approach with questions or concerns, and making time to properly answer questions and provide information to patients, visitors, and even staff. A good first impression means having the security officer stand on post. It demonstrates engagement as well as a friendly, inviting first impression. When a security officer is sitting behind a desk with their head down reading a book or newspaper, they demonstrate to patients and visitors their lack of caring. When patients or visitors ask a question and security officers seem bothered by the question or cannot answer it, they demonstrate a lack of caring. To provide attentiveness and presence, officers posted in entrances should stand in the path of travel, not off to the side, and make appropriate greetings and eye contact. Officers need to face their customers at all times. During low-volume times, officers in lobbies should step toward patients and visitors as they enter the hospital in order to provide them with a personalized greeting. During busy times, officers need to provide a general greeting to all persons entering and then make eye contact so that persons needing assistance see the officer's attentiveness. Officers should always remember to take the time to say thank you when patients and visitors are leaving. This process provides a solid security presence, along with a friendly caring exchange with patients and visitors.

Dignity and Respect

In all interactions, even during patient restraints or arrests, it is important to treat everyone with respect and dignity. Security staff should always communicate compassionately, and understand the cultural differences between themselves and the patients, visitors, and staff. Present a positive attitude toward the diversity of patients, visitors, and staff. Officers should understand and be trained on other's values, practices, and beliefs. For training it is important to find hospital staff members that are from the cultures that the hospital serves and have those persons attend security customer service training in order to explain the cultural differences and how best to greet and handle those cultures.

Staff interaction should be caring and affirming. Security staff should listen intently and be empathetic to the patient's or visitor's situation and needs. Remember the patient's point of view. Officers should apologize for poor service or mistakes and fix them whenever the officer or security staff is in a position to do so. Never underestimate the importance of officer appearance. It shows respect and engagement. Officers need to dress appropriately and maintain a consistent look. They need to make sure that their ID is in plain view. Security officers should always act in a professional manner: smile, be in proper uniform, maintain eye contact, and always have a positive attitude.

Communication

Communication means listening intently and being empathetic. Officers need to be able to give correct directions the same way every time, know operating hours for all clinics and doctor's offices, know the visiting policy, and know what to do when an employee enters the hospital without an ID. Directions should be spoken clearly and in plain language. Officers need to create that positive first impression by smiling, making good eye contact, having a happy upbeat attitude, and making sure the environment around them creates a positive impression as well.

Officers need to know what to say. Their message should be consistent. They should verbally welcome patients and visitors with a positive, friendly message and not forget to say thank you as patients and visitors are leaving. Using the right words when communicating helps to convey the correct message to patients, visitors, and staff. Positive customer service is all about what words are used when representing the hospital. What you say and how you say it can make a difference in how patients, visitors, and staff perceive security and the hospital. The message should cover basic questions that a patient or visitor might ask. Scripting should be used to designate general dialogue and certain engagement and courtesy guidelines. The security department should decide what phrases they would like their officers to say and in what situations they would like them to say the phrases. Each phrase should allow for the officer's personal touch. For example, all officers should have a greeting that opens dialogue, like "Good morning" or "Good evening," and stay away from phrases like "How are you?" Phrases such as "Welcome to X Hospital" are more open and set the tone of a welcoming, caring institution. The actual words should be the officer's own. As studies have indicated, it is important that each individual officer use their own words when addressing patients, visitors, and staff. This provides a more personal touch, again exhibiting that feeling of caring and calm. Spontaneity should be part of the script process so that it keeps the dialogue natural. When security officers are in tune with the purpose of the script and the desired response, they can freely use their own words and actions. Officers should speak courteously, respectfully, and enthusiastically in order to nurture open dialogue and build rapport. Add phrases that convey empathy and genuine concern for the patient's point of view and end every patient, visitor, or staff interaction with phrases that leave a positive impression in the customer's mind. Generally, a "Good morning," "Good afternoon," or "Good evening" is appropriate. Officers should then ask how they can help each individual and provide some basic information that would help individuals maneuver through the hospital. For example, explain how to get to the inpatient elevators or preadmission testing. Most importantly, officers should thank all patients and visitors for using the hospital's services and choosing that hospital. When dealing with difficult people, officers should be trained to maintain a professional image and communicate in a clear and precise manner. Conversation and instructions should be in simple language in order to reduce the opportunity for confusion by the patient or visitor. When speaking, officers should use a low, calming tone and not raise their voice.

Courtesy/Manners

One of the most important aspects of customer service is an officer's professionalism. Whether dealing with a difficult person or greeting persons as they enter the hospital, it is important to exhibit proper manners and courtesy. Maintaining that professional persona helps patients and visitors feel comfortable and secure within the hospital. Courtesy and manners means greeting everyone with an offer of assistance and thanking them for using the hospital's services. It means offering to hold open the door or assisting individuals as they are stepping up or down a stair, or even assisting people into and out of a car. Officers should be as verbal as possible when carrying out their duties, again establishing that personal rapport. Phrases like "Let me get the door for you" or "Let me help you" should be encouraged. Officers should also remember to say "Thank you," "Excuse me," or "I am sorry" when appropriate. Officers should always be courteous in all situations, even the most grievous, like being struck or spit upon. Early in my career, an employee spit in the face of one of the security officers that I supervised when she refused entry to the employee for not having their ID card. This officer remained calm, wiped the spit off her face, and called for backup. Even after the employee was caught and called her names, she remained calm. After the event, I asked her how she did it. She stated that she knew that he would be appropriately punished for his actions, so she saw no need to overreact to the situation. That is real professionalism, and just so that you know the conclusion to the story, the employee was immediately terminated by our CEO.

Responsiveness

Responsiveness means educating and allowing officers and supervisors to have the freedom, flexibility, and understanding of their job in order to respond to situations within their immediate work area. Officer posts and patrols should be geared toward having the flexibility to either fix mistakes when they occur or pass them on to another staff member. Officers should have the freedom to make decisions and handle situations as they arise, relying on supervision only in difficult situations, having the flexibility to assist patients, visitors, or even staff, to provide a security image that demonstrates engagement and responsiveness.

Consistent Service

The security department should be in an environment that encourages employees to provide consistent service. Customer service research indicates the need for consistent service. That means working together to provide consistent service within and across service lines and within all posts and shifts of the security department. One of the marks of a world-class organization, as mentioned in Fred Lee's book, is its ability to repeat a performance over and over with the same consistency. Each officer should provide the same level of service every day. To achieve true consistency, security staff should know the hospital and the rules, the location of all services and doctor's offices, and their hours of operation. Security staff should know the rules for visitation for patient visitors and staff, and know the policy for vendors and construction workers, along with any other policies relating to visitation. They need to know how to enforce the rules and the appropriate response to situations involving rule violations or exceptions. There should be a system in place to check the quality of an officer's work to further ensure consistent service. Issues or problems that develop at the end of a tour should not be dropped but picked up and resolved by the incoming tour. When a complaint or problem occurs, it is important that the issue be handed off to a person that can fix it. Make sure that an issue is followed up and resolved when handed off.

Last Word on Customer Service

In Fred Lee's book, he uses several examples that demonstrate poor service. Unfortunately, his examples used security personnel and exemplify the need for customer service within security on all levels. Fred Lee's first story talks about a training class in the early morning. Upon Fred's arrival and the arrival of others, they find the classroom door locked. He goes on to explain his encounter with security as follows:

> We called security. A security officer arrived with a passkey but insisted that he did not have the authority to open the room.

Lee commented, "But you can see we are all ready for the class. Weren't you in this class yesterday?" "Yes, I know," answered the security officer. "But I am not allowed to open a room without permission to do so from central dispatch." "Maybe there is somebody in administration by now," Lee ventured. "That won't do any good," the officer said. "I don't take orders from administration. I have to call my dispatch office, which is across town at the main hospital. Until they tell me to open the classroom, I can't, I'm really sorry."

Fred goes on to tell another story from the same hospital system described by an executive who had a doctor leave something in the medical library, but even she could not get "the guy from security," who she knew very well, to open the door so the doctor could get his stuff. The security officer stated that he had to wait for orders from their central office across town.

In Lee's third example, he was working as an administrator on call and received a call from a physician who was upset. The physician explained how he had been called in on his day off by the emergency department to assess a critical case. As he was leaving, his car ran out of gas in the emergency room parking lot. The doctor said, "Nobody seems to be able to give me a hand. I tried security, but the guy says he is the only one here and can't reach his boss to get permission to leave the premises and take me to a nearby gas station. The operator then paged the engineer on call, and he took forever to come down, only to say it was not his job. He said he thought that was security's job." The doctor's comment, "Can't anybody around here perform a simple act of helpfulness?" Fred then gave the security officer permission to leave the facility, get a container from engineering, get the doctor gas, and give the receipt to Fred so he could reimburse the security officer.

Fred calls this behavior "functional silo," which gives frontline employees only the ability to say no, leaving only the people at the top of the silo with the authority to say yes.

The authority to say yes elevates the status of every employee. A major contributor to burnout is a feeling that one has no control over one's work. Being unable to make decisions, unable to please a patient or the family member without permission, unable to do anything but pass on complaints, is debilitating and discouraging. It becomes even worse when managers insist that their employees say no, only to overrule the employee when the complaint comes to them. Think how demoralizing it must be for the security officer to be unable to perform a simple task spontaneously, especially if 10 minutes later he is instructed to do the thing he would have done anyway, only now he looks stupid and ineffective to the customer. Multiply this embarrassment and lack of autonomy by many events in a day and we are faced with the turnover of excellent employees.[8]

References

1. Centers for Medicare & Medicaid Services. *HCAHPS: Patients' Perspectives of Care Survey.* https://www.cms.gov/Medicare/Quality-Initiatives-Patient-Assessment-Instruments/HospitalQualityInits/HospitalHCAHPS.html.
2. J.D. Power and Associates. *Patient Satisfaction Influenced More by Hospital Staff than by the Hospital Facilities* September 2012. www.jdpower.com/business/press-releases/2012-national-patient-experience-study.
3. Rozenblum, Ronen. Patient experience and patient-centered care—do we really care? *Journal of Postdoctoral Research*, Vol. 1, No. 10, pp.11–14. 2013.
4. Toma, Ghazwan, Wayne Triner, and Louise-Ann McNutt. *The Practice of Emergency Medicine/Original Research, Patient Satisfaction as a Function of Emergency Department Previsit Expectations.* Albany, NY: Albany Medical College, Department of Emergency Medicine (Triner), University at Albany, School of Public Health.
5. Koichiro, Otani, Brian Waterman, Kelly M. Faulkner, Sarah Boslaugh, Thomas E. Burroughs, and Claiborne W. Dunagan. Patient satisfaction: Focusing on "excellent". *Journal of Healthcare Management*, Vol. 54, No. 2, pp. 93–103. 2009.
6. Torcson, Patrick J. Patient satisfaction: The hospitalist's role. *The Hospitalist*, Vol. 7, 2005.
7. Goodman, John. Manage complaints to enhance loyalty. *Quality Progress*, Vol. 39, No. 2, 8–34, 2006.
8. Lee, Fred. *If Disney Ran Your Hospital: 9½ Things You Would Do Differently.* Bozeman, MT: Second River Healthcare Press, 2004.
9. Mastrofski, Stephen D. *Ideas in American Policing: Policing for People.* Washington, DC: Police Foundation, March 1999.
10. Tyler, Tom. *Why People Obey the Law.* New Haven: Yale University Press, 1990.

Chapter 8

Predictive Analytics: Metrics Use and Evaluation

Introduction

A "metric" is defined as a statistical relationship between variables within the management process. It is a statistical measure of performance, process, or product—a tool that determines variation and relationship between variables within the management process. In the security field, metrics monitor security survey compliance, determine failure rates in physical security systems, increase emergency response time, identify criminal behaviors and trends, increase a security officer's job function efficiencies, and improve staff job satisfaction. The use of metrics provides a knowledge base that:

- Increases efficiency of operations and finances
- Provides for a better-quality service
- Allows the security department to compete for continually limited resources
- Better aligns the department with the company's strategic mission and goals

Metrics not only monitor the quality of services provided, but also uncover information never considered important in the transformation to a highly efficient, performance-driven organization. The development and implementation of a metrics-based data collection and analysis program is essential for today's security department. Every security department should be collecting data as part of its quality performance program. The collection of data specific to a metrics-based program incorporates the innermost workings of the security department, focusing on job process and levels of completion or success. From a metrics perspective, data collection should include completion rates, failure rates, satisfaction levels, and process flow. For a security department, metrics include calls for service, incident data, customer service levels, security survey compliance/noncompliance, security officer job satisfaction, and job processes including scheduling, post duties, meal and break relief, and overtime usage.

In the case of a metrics-based program it's the expansion of the data collection process that is most important. Metrics goes beyond standard data collection utilizing surveys and audits to analyze job functions. For example, although it is important to document the number of times a task is completed, a metrics-based program is concerned with documenting the time frequency, start to finish, or analyzing the value of the service provided. In addition, a metrics-based program is also interested in the satisfaction level of the service provided. Data is collected in two forms: continuous and discrete. Discrete data is represented by a count or the number of times it occurs. This is the easiest analysis for metric generation. The most common and useful discrete indicator is sorting. Sorting allows for the analysis of frequency. Frequency shows the highest number of times a task occurs. Data can also be analyzed to determine mean, average, and standard deviation. Continuous data denotes data that is time based. Time interval can be collected and analyzed to show the longest period, the shortest time period, the mean, the average, and the standard deviation. Other discrete data includes task satisfaction and task value. Satisfaction relates to the end user's feelings about how the job task was done and completed and their treatment during the process. Job value has to do with a breakdown of the task and analysis to determine efficiencies, ways to make the task easier and/or cheaper, or whether the task should be done at all.

The most common data analysis tool used is frequency/percent of occurrence and highest value recorded. These measures help determine where and how resources are being utilized. Once data is analyzed, it needs to be evaluated against comparative data. Data can be compared with internal or external data sources. Externally, data comparisons are called benchmarking, comparing a task with the same task at similar institutions. Internal comparisons are conducted with other hospital departments or comparisons internal to the department. Data is compared with that from prior months to look for developing trends and patterns.

Starting a Metrics-Based Program

Utilizing metrics provides a quantifiable way to measure the effectiveness of security programs and processes. As the popularity of utilizing metrics has increased over the past few years, so has the number and type of metrics that are used to evaluate efficiencies. However, without proper vetting metrics may not effectively evaluate the process or program that is being measured. Metrics must be chosen carefully to ensure that they measure exactly what they were intended to measure. Many times, when evaluating programs or processes, metrics are used that do not measure the program and have nothing to do with evaluating a program's effectiveness. When choosing metrics, care must be taken to ensure that they offer a true measurement and that the measurement they provide is relevant to the improvement of the process or program. The determination of the most effective metrics has been debated for many years and by many organizations, and individuals have offered their own version of metrics that demonstrate efficiency or value in healthcare security. Some of these metrics include:

- Officer response time to emergent situations
- The number of security department–generated incident reports presented monthly or weekly
- The amount of reported crime presented within a specific period, like monthly or weekly
- The number of calls for security service over a given period
- The institution's square footage

Some institutions compare security-specific metrics to hospital-based metrics so that senior management can better relate to the security program, for example, connecting the security incident rate to patient length of stay or bed census.

The metrics determination process starts with the program purpose, scope, or any goals associated with the program, and a breakdown of the program functions. For example, when evaluating visitor screening services, effective metrics may be:

- The average length of time a person waits for a pass
- The number of passes issued in a specific time frame
- The results of a security audit on how many visitors surveyed were wearing their pass opposed to the number that were not

- The number of passes issued each day, week, or month
- The number of persons that enter each post, broken down by time period
- The time it takes to produce a pass for each visitor

These are all metrics that can help in the determination of effectiveness that is specific to the security program or the specific security task of issuing visitor passes.

Metrics look to compare best practices, user satisfaction, and process efficiencies. This is done through nontraditional statistical analysis, variation, relationship, and value analysis. Every function conducted by the security department should be documented. Manpower statistics should be collected and analyzed. Each post, patrol, and job completed in the security department equates to time. A post is manned so many hours a day, week, or year. Patrols take so many hours a day. This time data should be collected and used to compare lost time—sick hours, nonpaid hours, and late hours. This data shows manpower efficiencies when compared with the total number of hours the department works. Sick time or lateness can be benchmarked either internally, with other departments within the company, or outside the company, with other security departments within the same industry and of the same size.

Now that metrics have been set up and are monitoring department measures, one area to consider is the reduction in determined high-frequency areas. The next step in the development and implementation of a metric-based management system is to look at ways to reduce high-frequency rates. Data sorted in a database will indicate categories of high-frequency occurrence, which may be identified as needing to be reduced in order to improve security services. The best example of frequency analysis is with incident data. Collecting and segregating type of incidents; occurrence based on time of day, day of the week, and month; location; and the names of victims and perpetrators provides insight into the most frequent occurrence rates. Rates can be reduced by focusing resources on the most frequent locations, types, and times of occurrence. This process provides a more efficient use of manpower and department resources in the reduction of crime.

A Metrics-Based Program in Action

The implementation of a metrics-based program relies on the collection and analysis of unconventional data—data that stresses success rates, error rates, satisfaction levels, and the percent of time spent completing a task. The development and implementation of the metrics-based program provides increased customer service and efficiencies within the security department.

Collect data on all facets of security operations. Utilize the data to facilitate decisions on manpower placement, services provided to the hospital, capital budget allocations, training initiatives, and investigations. Through the institution of simple analytical techniques, the security program can be effectively evaluated. The best process for data evaluation utilizes methods where data is easy to collect and simple to analyze. The process of collection and analysis requires:

1. The creation of data collection tools
2. The development of a process for the evaluation of different types of collected data
3. The integration of data collection analysis into the management of security operations
4. The development of a process to ensure that data is collected and analyzed consistently and on a continuous basis

The data collection process utilizes three methods to collect data: interviews, audits, and tally sheets. These simple tools are used to survey staff, to conduct security audits, to benchmark with other professionals, and to calculate specific department activities.

Interviews are conducted to collect data about specific aspects of the security program or to obtain a general overview of the security services provided to the hospital. Interviews allow for the analysis of the security program from the perspective of the end user. For example, survey questions are designed to initiate discussions on property loss, security officer posting or response, physical security systems in place or being planned, and security problems the end user has encountered. In addition, previous security recommendations made to the department can be reviewed to determine if they were implemented. If not, other recommendations can be explored with the end user during the interview process. Annually, the security department should survey department heads, senior administrators, and employees. These annual interviews are conducted in a number of areas throughout the hospital. Areas or departments are surveyed based on risk factors. Areas within the hospital are rated as high risk through interviews, benchmarking audits, and tally sheet data. Interviews are also conducted to benchmark. Benchmarking through interviewing means developing and maintaining a relationship with several peers or experts in the field to periodically exchange information on problems and programs. The information obtained through benchmarking is helpful in collecting data and developing solutions to problems. Benchmarking interviews include discussions on current or previous security problems, security programs in place, and solutions to problems that have been implemented. Besides interviews, benchmarking is used to compare tallied data. Compare data on crime incidents, patient watches, and specific property crimes, like computer thefts. Benchmarking also includes collecting information through written literature. Written material such as local newspaper articles and industry-specific publications are reviewed on a regular basis. Publications offer information about specific types of incidents that have occurred, potential high-risk situations, and effective security programs.

During an interview, benchmarking session, or review of written literature, specific data is collected and recorded for the analysis process. Short snippets of information are documented that highlight and/or summarize problems discussed, data comparisons, problem solutions, and information on security practices or procedures. In addition to the snippet of information, the time the information was collected, the date it was collected, the source of the collected data, the department or area involved, and the interviewee are recorded.

Security audits provide key data for the metrics program. A team of staff within the security department, usually an investigator, a physical security specialist, and a locksmith, conduct the audits. The team performs a physical inspection of the surveyed area and interviews staff about the specific security problems they encountered. After the walk-through, the team identifies specific security problems and makes recommendations to resolve the identified problems. Audits are initiated by the security department for a number of reasons: a high rate of incident reports for an area or department, literature indicating a current or emerging concern or event, or a manager or administrator requesting an audit be conducted. The survey team documents a short summary on the scope of the audit, the specific findings of the survey team, and some suggested recommendations relating to each of the findings. In addition to each finding and recommended solution, the team records the time and date of the survey, the department or area the survey was conducted in, and the name of a contact person for follow-up or questions.

The most common data collection tool utilized is the tally sheet. It is the simplest and most effective form of data collection. Tally sheets count values for particular data that is being collected. For example, when determining the total number of patrols conducted during a 24-hour period, the security staff can place a mark on a sheet of paper each time a patrol is completed. The marks can be totaled at the end of the day to determine the number of patrols conducted during the past 24 hours. The specific number of patrols conducted on each tour or the locations of each patrol can be tallied as well. The security department utilizes tally sheets to determine department calls for service, personnel activity and usage, and incident report data. For incident data, regardless of the type of incident—a missing purse or a person who fell on the sidewalk—incident reports are tallied by the day the incident occurred, the shift the incident occurred on, the location the incident occurred in, and the type of incident that occurred. In order to be thorough in the data collection process, even the most insignificant events should be documented. A report of items moved around in an office is as important as the theft of a video recorder or other valuable. In addition to incident report data, department activity data should be collected. As an example, security should tally requests to open doors, persons calling and asking for directions, the number of patrols conducted by officers, and the number of officer posts inspected. This information should be recorded on a tally sheet to total all of the calls for service that the department responds to during each tour of duty. The tour sheets are then totaled at the end of each month and the monthly data is analyzed.

Information pertaining to personnel is collected for analysis as well. Tally sheets collect data on sick time usage, overtime hours, and any other information that shows an exception to the officers working. Daily, the department totals the number of hours required to man all officer posts, patrols, and special assignments. This number is compared with the amount of sick time hours, holiday hours, vacation time, disability time, and any other time that keeps an officer from working. The officer's time not working is compared with the total number of hours for the shift, which creates a number representing the percentage of the total work hours. These percentages are compared monthly and yearly to determine patterns or trends in time off.

The security department conducts focus surveys when additional information is needed on specific data collected on the tally sheets. Focus surveys provide more detailed information on specific data collected. For example, when the number of door opening calls is considered high, a focus survey can be implemented. The survey records the start time and completion time for the call, the location of the call, the person requesting the call, and the reason for the call.

In order for the data collection and analysis program to be successful, all of the data should be collected consistently and in a continuous manner.

The process of data collection is never ending and should be incorporated into all facets of security operations. Interviews and audits should be conducted throughout the year. The information gathered from the interviews and audits should be collected by one person. This person records the information and prepares it for analysis. Tally sheets are completed on a daily basis. This data, as well, should be processed by one person in the department and prepared for analysis.

Data Analysis

The security department should utilize only one tool to analyze the data it collects: frequency of occurrence. Those items with the highest frequency of occurrence present concentrations or "hot spots" that are worth investigating further. High-frequency data should also be compared with data from previous months and years to determine trends or patterns.

All of the collected data to be analyzed should be placed in an Excel spreadsheet for analysis. The analysis process starts with the tally sheet data. Tally sheets should be completed during each tour and then totaled at the end of each month for analysis. Call for service data should be sorted by call frequency. The sorted data reveals the calls with the highest number of occurrences. The top five categories are then highlighted for further analysis. The next group of data to be sorted is incident report data. This data is placed on the spreadsheet and sorted by location, type, shift, and day of the week. When sorted, the data shows the most frequent location of occurrence, incident type, shift of occurrence, and day of the week of occurrence. This data is compared with that from other months and years to determine patterns or trends. Personnel data is not sorted but divided into the total number of hours that officers are scheduled to work for the month. For example, if 10 officers are assigned to every 8-hour shift 24 hours a day, 7 days a week, they are on duty 1,680 hours a week. If four officers call in sick for two shifts during that month, they were sick 64 hours or 4% of the total hours worked. Interview and audit data are sorted as well. Then the like items are counted and the ones that appear the most frequently in the sort are analyzed. This data is sorted by location, identified problem, and interviewee. The frequency of occurrence is not as prevalent as in the tally sheet data, but the process provides information that supports other findings and provides some solutions to the problems identified throughout this process.

The next step in the process is to take all of the identified high-frequency data and sort it by location of occurrence and problem type. In most cases, the data does not need to be sorted on a spreadsheet. Eyeing the data identifies the highest-occurring locations and problem types. This data should be reviewed monthly and compared with that from prior months and years. The comparison is conducted to denote patterns and trends in the data. Again, as the department compares each month's data, a pattern forms highlighting the most frequent locations and problems. This is the data that is used to make decisions regarding officer placement, services provided to the hospital, training initiatives, and investigations. Security resources should be concentrated in the areas that appear most frequently in the analysis. In addition to identifying the most frequent locations and problems, evaluate each high-frequency occurrence to look at the reason behind the high-frequency volume. Looking at the details of each event to further breakdown data in order to determine the cause.[1]

Examples of Success

A focus survey was conducted on requests to security to unlock doors. The department felt that this activity, although necessary, takes too much time away from patrols and other more important security functions. The department's call for service tally sheet recorded an average of 400 door openings monthly. Being one of the top requested service calls, the department decided it needed to further analyze the reason and need for these calls. To determine the reason for this high usage of manpower, the department developed and implemented a detailed tally sheet specifically for door opening calls. When a call was made to open a door, the security dispatcher would record the person's name, the location of the door, the reason for opening the door, and the start and end time for the call. This data was collected for several months and then it was sorted by location and by the person making the request. The highest-frequency locations were visited, and the highest-frequency persons were contacted to determine why the calls were made. As a result of the analysis, it was determined that a small group of employees represented the majority of the calls. The calls were made because employees either left their keys home or lost their keys. Staff would call security each morning and evening to open and lock their offices. To reduce the number of calls, the identified persons were issued keys to their offices and work sites. As a result, door opening calls dropped by several hundred a month. This increased the number of patrols conducted each day and kept the meal break schedule on time.

The number of calls from people requesting directions to the hospital was questioned by a senior administrator who was reviewing department data. The senior administrator was reviewing security department data because of several complaints by other departments that the security dispatchers were not timely in their phone call pickup and that callers were frequently being placed on hold. The security department received approximately 300–400 calls each month. At the administrator's request, a focus survey was conducted on calls for directions. The survey documented the start and end time of each call, the time of day for each call, the town the person lived in, the person's name, and a brief description of the directions given to the caller. The start and end times were collected to see exactly how much time was spent answering direction calls. The time of day was collected to see if an additional dispatcher was needed during certain hours of the day. Towns were recorded to see if a marketing campaign needed be done. The description was documented to see if any pattern developed in staff responses and whether training was needed for the dispatchers. Also, repeat callers were tracked to see if special information could be sent to them by mail or through their visits to the hospital. After several months of data collection, the following was found. The majority of calls came from three specific towns, the towns immediately surrounding the hospital. There was no pattern relating to the person's name, the time of the call, or the direction description. As a result of the focus survey, it was decided to benchmark with other hospitals to see what they do with calls for directions. An interview sheet was developed, and specific questions were asked. The interviews determined that all competitors utilized automated directions. The automated directions were part of their automated phone directory. Directions were listed at the end of the main menu. Either the automated directions were placed at the end of the phone menu or the caller had to go through several levels in the phone menu system to reach the directions prompt. The survey also asked if the hospitals had received any feedback on their automated directions. Most of the hospitals indicated that people were unhappy with automated directions. They said that the directions were incomplete and difficult to reach and could not be repeated, and callers had to hang up, redial, and ask the operator if they needed more detailed directions. As a result of the interviews and data collection, directions were placed at the beginning of the main phone menu. The directions could be repeated by pressing a designated key, and at the end of the direction announcement the caller could press a key to be automatically transferred to the security department. When transferred, the caller could speak to a security dispatcher—an option no other hospital had. Calls for directions continued to be tracked for several months after the installation of the automated directions. The department averaged only 10–20 calls each month, a reduction of more than 200%. The dispatchers now had more time to respond to more important calls.

After reviewing personnel data, the security department analyzed overtime and sick time data, the two highest-frequency items. An initial analysis of the two was conducted. It showed that overtime and sick time were related. Overtime rates were high to cover for officers out sick. The security department was running a 12% sick time rate. Dividing the total number of officer sick time hours into the total number of hours all security officers worked derived this number. Through officer interviews it was determined that staff not having daycare for their kids caused the highest percentage of sick time. Many suggestions by the officers were reviewed to provide a solution to the overtime problem. The department decided to try 12½-hour work tours for all security officers. This allowed the officers to work only three days a week. This process reduced sick time to less than 1%.

The most significant example of the benefits to data collection and analysis is illustrated from the analysis of incident report data. The security reports were reviewed for all of the incidents that occurred in the building for a period of one year. The most frequent incident type was property crime. These reports were evaluated to determine the type of property that was taken. After reviewing several years of data and interviewing staff and patients, it was determined that cash, eyeglasses, and dentures represented the vast majority of lost property. The security department initiated a program to reduce the number of property incidents that occurred. First, the department determined why patients keep cash with them during their stay. The answer was to pay for TV service. Meetings were held with the TV rental service, resulting in the elimination of cash collections. A process was implemented to have patients pay for service either by credit card or up front as a debit account. Second, training sessions were conducted with nursing and laundry staff to emphasize the need to watch out for eyeglasses and dentures. Third, a new brighter denture cup was purchased for patient use, and safes for valuables were installed at nursing stations to safeguard patients' belongings, including eyeglasses. The results of security's efforts reduced the number of property incidents in the inpatient building by 70% over a three-year period.

Financial Value

Evaluating incident rate, crime rate, service calls, and officer response does establish value for the security program. Alternatively, demonstrating value can also be about the effectiveness of these services in relation to their monetary value to the organization, or it can be about the perception of security that is felt by patients, visitors, and staff. The value of the security program can be determined by how security officers perform their duties compared with the costs associated with the program and how patients, visitors, and staff perceive the security program as it relates to them feeling safe and secure. These two metrics are often not utilized in the evaluation of value and should be considered when demonstrating the true worth of the security program and its effectiveness in providing a safe and secure environment. What does it cost the hospital to provide security services, and how effective are the services compared with their cost? By attaching a cost to security services and evaluating the effectiveness of those services, value to the hospital for those services can be determined. Individual programs like patrol, visitor screening, employee escort, or patient restraints can be reviewed to determine the individual cost to provide those services. Then individual metrics related to that service can be developed to help measure the program's effectiveness. Together, both metrics demonstrate the value of security programs to the hospital. Using a cost metric allows for an evaluation based on a quantifiable number that the C-suite can understand.

Determining program financial value starts with the definition of services. Property collection, patrol, visitor screening, etc., must be reviewed to determine purpose and scope; then the labor and operational costs can be established. Costs can be determined by the average salary of the officers assigned to the particular task or program. If the same officers hold a specific job regularly, then their actual salary can be used. For service calls, the average officer's salary is assigned to the call for the time associated with that service.

Next is determining the effectiveness of the program. When all the metrics that show effectiveness are gathered, they need to be compared with the program's expense. This comparison will determine service value to the hospital. As an example, if an entrance is staffed with two officers from noon to 8:00 p.m. at an average expense of $50 an hour, and from 12:00 to 4:00 p.m. 20 visitors are screened, then the total expense to screen visitors is $200 or $10 per visitor. From 4:00 to 8:00 p.m. 100 visitors are screened; then the expense is $2 per visitor. However, if the wait time for a pass from 4:00 to 8:00 p.m. is five minutes, but at 12:00 to 4:00 p.m. it is one minute, then the value of the service changes. From 4:00 to 8:00 p.m. the expenses are lower but the service metric is higher, resulting in a lower-value service. From this example, it can be determined that visitor screening has a lower customer value from 4:00 to 8:00 p.m. when lines are long compared with 12:00 to 4:00 p.m. when lines are short. This example shows how financial evaluation can demonstrate value as well as help to identify potential service issues. For this program, it might be better to even out the costs by reducing to one officer from 12:00 to 4:00 p.m. and having three officers from 4:00 to 8:00 p.m. For this example, the expense from noon to 4:00 p.m. would now be $25 an hour or $100 for the four hours, or $5 per visitor. From 4:00 to 8:00 p.m. the expense for the officers would be $75 an hour or $300 for the four hours, or $3 per visitor. Screening time increased to about two minutes from noon to 4:00 p.m. and decreased to two minutes from 4:00 to 8:00 p.m. Now, the cost of the screening program from 12:00 to 8:00 p.m. is $400, with an average cost of $3.50 per visitor. Screening time now averages two minutes.

The true value of developing and monitoring services by expense compared with service is when budget reduction or program evaluation is needed. For example, if security is asked to decrease their budget by a specific amount of money, then service changes can be evaluated from a financial perspective. The security department can save $700 a week by eliminating the third screening officer from 4:00 to 8:00 p.m. daily. This will decrease the cost per visitor from $3 to $2 but increase waiting time from two minutes to five minutes.

Perception of Security

It is well known in the security industry that the perception of security can be different from the actual amount of security that is present. However, perception many times dictates security service placement. The perception of poor security, insecurity, or fear often takes precedent over a strategically placed security program. The perception of security tends to be reactive, as opposed to planned or evaluated service execution. Because perception can be such a strong driver of service placement, it is important to monitor perception so that service changes can be anticipated as opposed to being reactive. Monitoring the feelings or perceptions of patients, visitors, and staff regarding security has value in determining the effectiveness of security services.

How can perception be measured? It can be measured in several different ways, but mainly it should be accomplished through survey. Ask patients, visitors, and staff, on a regular basic, how safe they feel at their work location and in the hospital overall. Surveys should be short and to the point, asking only a few questions at a time, like: How safe do you feel in the hospital? How safe do you feel in your workplace or patient room? How safe do you feel visiting at night or after 8:00 p.m.? Do you feel safe walking to your car at night? A survey should be limited to two or three questions at a time and should use a rating scale or yes/no answer. A comment area should be made available so that patients, visitors, or staff can give examples of why they feel or do not feel safe. Surveys can be conducted by email, by mail, or in person. For patients and visitors, it is best to conduct surveys in person while they are on site so that information is obtained in a timely fashion and response rates are higher.

Perception can also be determined by the number of service calls for a specific hospital location: department or nursing unit. High rates of specific types of calls may indicate a perception of poor security or a higher feeling of insecurity by patients, visitors, or staff. For example, a high number of calls for disruptive patients or visitors to a nursing unit may indicate the perception of insecurity, or visitors and staff may have more fear compared with units that do not have a high rate of disruptive patients or visitors. Perception can be determined by the number of incident reports generated for specific departments or nursing units. Additional metrics may include the number of exterior lights not working in a specific location at night, the number of broken doors locks at any given time, the length of time between when a broken door is reported and then repaired, and the number of escorts provided at night to parked cars or bus stops.

Perception is another metric that can be compared with security services like escorts or physical security installations of CCTV. Perception can also be compared with the overall crime rate, incident report rate, or any other metric. Service and perception comparisons help to determine the value of security services demonstrating the value of the service from the eyes of the patient, visitor, and staff.[2]

Metrics-Based Risk Assessment

Metrics-based assessments utilize data to determine high-risk areas and risk probabilities. Unlike traditional assessments, which rely on physically surveying the hospital to pinpoint inadequacies within the current security program, metrics-based analysis highlights data to illustrate avenues for improvement. A metrics-based assessment provides the security director with a view of the immediate and strategic concerns as well as an organized perspective to help mitigate risk in the future. A metrics-based assessment starts with the determination of high-risk or security-sensitive areas. This data is obtained through the analysis of:

- Incident data review
- Benchmarking with like hospitals
- Literature review of organizational publications
- Calls for service data
- Complaint data
- Staff and patient survey data
- Self-reporting survey data
- Industry standards and guidelines

Once analyzed, the data will yield categories to be developed that identify specific areas for improvement. Then those high-risk or security-sensitive areas can be surveyed and assessed to determine what methods for improvement will be most effective.

For example, incident and call for service data can be broken down by incident demographics, i.e., time of day, incident type, day of the week, and victim type. Benchmarking data identifies problems other hospitals may be experiencing. Another source of data important to the assessment includes self-reporting surveys. Surveys should be developed specifically for each high-risk area and administered to staff, patients, and visitors. Questions should request general information on the security of the area, like how safe they feel, or do they have security concerns? Then more specific questions can be asked that relate to the data collected identifying specific areas of concern.

Once all the data is collected, it should be reviewed by an assessment team. This team should comprise key stakeholders within the identified areas of risk, along with security and senior administrative personnel. The purpose of the team is to review the data and develop recommendations to improve the overall quality of the security program. Important to the metrics-based assessment is the implementation of recommended solutions.

Data acts as a baseline in determining the effectiveness of resolutions and proven quality improvement metrics for the security program, which is a language that is better understood by the C-suite and senior management. Are you more likely to obtain $20,000 for a visitor management system for woman's health by presenting senior management with an anecdotal statement that your staff feels insecure or by presenting empirical data that includes incident reports, calls for response, and industry guidelines that document the risk of unauthorized visitors entering the maternity unit? Additionally, monies allocated to the visitor management project can be further justified by trending its long-term effectiveness through lower incident and call rates documented over time.

To conduct a thorough and complete assessment, major resources must be committed to the project over a long period of time. Because of this required commitment, consideration should be given to utilizing a third-party provider/consultant who understands the metrics-based assessment process. Working as a team, data collection and analysis can be conducted by the consultant, while recommendations can be developed through the in-house assessment team. This allows the security director to focus on appropriate resolutions. Recommendations determined by the assessment team can then be documented by the consultant and given to the security department to present to the C-suite. Follow-up can also be conducted by the consultant providing trended data to the security director that demonstrates quality improvement in the security program over time.

References

1. Scaglione, Bernard J. and Anthony J. Luizzo An alternative view in the development of healthcare security metrics. *Journal of Healthcare Protection Management*, Vol. 31, No. 2, pp. 98–104, 2015.
2. Scaglione, Bernard J. and Anthony J. Luizzo. Applying metrics to 21st century healthcare security. *Journal of Healthcare Protection Management*, Vol. 33, No. 2, pp. 7–13. 2017.

Chapter 9

Violence Prevention

Introduction

Violence within hospitals is a foreseeable event. No hospital is immune from the possibility of a violent event. A strong violence prevention program implemented throughout the hospital can dramatically reduce the likelihood of a violent event. The Joint Commission (TJC) requires hospitals to annually assess their security risks by identifying security-sensitive (high-risk) areas and to assess the effectiveness of the security program. In June 2010, the Joint Commission issued Sentinel Event Alert Number 45; this required all hospitals to conduct a workplace violence assessment and track any improvements developed out of that assessment. There are other professional organizations that have published guidelines relative to workplace violence and risk assessments. These resources include:

- Occupational Safety and Health Administration (OSHA) Publication No. 3827
- Centers for Disease Control and Prevention (CDC)–National Institute for Occupational Safety and Health (NIOSH) Publication No. 2002–101
- International Association for Healthcare Security and Safety (IAHSS)— "Healthcare Security: Basic Industry Guidelines"
- ASIS International—"Workplace Violence Prevention and Response"
- ASIS Healthcare Council—"Managing Aggressive and Disruptive Behavior in Healthcare"

Reduction Resources

OSHA 3827, entitled "Preventing Workplace Violence: A Road Map for Healthcare Facilities," outlines prevention strategies for the reduction of violence in hospitals. These include evaluating the physical environment to provide barriers between staff and patients that keep patients from accessing staff when they become agitated or violent, implementing administrative controls to provide a work environment that reduces the opportunities for violence, and modifying staff and patient behaviors so that aggressive behavior can be identified early and handled in a way that reduces the opportunity for injury. Lastly, the OSHA publication provides basic safety tips for all employees to help them reduce the potential for violence while working within the healthcare environment.

OSHA 3827 identifies areas within the hospital that contain the highest risk for violence. These include:

- Psychiatric units
- The emergency department
- Geriatric units
- ICUs, pediatrics, and maternity
- Waiting rooms for the above-listed areas

OSHA recommends that all healthcare institutions that contain these departments conduct a risk assessment that includes the evaluation of the physical environment, review and implementation of administrative controls, and staff training in order for staff to recognize potential violence and be able to handle violent situations effectively. OHSA provides a checklist in order to assess high-risk areas. The checklist includes the identification of high-risk personnel and areas that are specific to the institution and based on quantifiable data like injury reports, worker lost day reports to OHSA, and any police or security reports that indicate violence within specific areas of the hospital. In addition, OSHA supports postoccurrence response and gathering data from those meetings to reduce the potential for violence. Collected data includes the identification of job categories and locations with the greatest risk to violence. From the resulting analysis, design measures should be implemented that incorporate:

- Engineering controls
- Administrative controls
- Training
- Practices and process for staff

OSHA suggests the inclusion of specific engineering controls in order to modify the physical environment. Engineering controls remove the hazard from the workplace or create a physical barrier between staff and patients. Some options to consider include:

■ Install and regularly maintain alarm systems and other security devices, panic buttons, handheld alarms or noise devices, cellular phones, and private channel radios.
■ Use a reliable response system that is triggered by an alarm.
■ Use metal detectors—installed or handheld, where appropriate—to detect guns, knives, or other weapons.
■ Use closed-circuit video recording for high-risk areas.
■ Use curved mirrors at hallway intersections or concealed areas.
■ Enclose the reception, triage, and admitting areas or client service rooms in resistant, shatterproof glass.
■ Provide employee "safe rooms" for use during emergencies.
■ Establish "time-out" or seclusion areas with high ceilings without grids for patients who "act out," and establish separate rooms for criminal patients.

OHSA also recommends that workplace violence reduction measures be part of the design and construction for any new or renovated spaces within the healthcare facility.

Administrative and work practice controls can affect the way staff perform jobs or tasks. Changes in work practices and administrative procedures can help prevent violent incidents. Some options for employers to consider include:

■ Clearly stating to patients, clients, and employees that violence is not permitted or tolerated
■ Establishing a liaison with local police and prosecutors
■ Giving police physical layouts of facilities to expedite response and investigations
■ Requiring all employees to report all assaults or threats to a supervisor or manager
■ Keeping logbooks and reports of such incidents to help determine any necessary actions to prevent recurrences
■ Advising employees of company procedures for requesting police assistance or filing charges when assaulted and helping them do so, if necessary

- Providing management support by responding promptly to all complaints
- Setting up a trained response team for emergency response
- Ensuring that adequate and properly trained staff are available to restrain patients or clients, if necessary
- Providing sensitive and timely information to people waiting in line or in waiting rooms
- Adopting measures to decrease waiting time

NIOSH Publication Number 2002-101, titled "Violence: Occupational Hazards in Hospitals," gives examples of risk factors that can contribute to violence within the healthcare setting. These risk factors include:

- Working directly with volatile people, especially if they are under the influence of drugs or alcohol or have a history of violence or certain psychotic diagnoses
- Working when understaffed—especially during mealtimes and visiting hours
- Transporting patients
- Long waits for service
- Overcrowded, uncomfortable waiting rooms
- Working alone
- Poor environmental design
- Inadequate security
- Lack of staff training and policies for preventing and managing crises with potentially volatile patients
- Access to firearms
- Poorly lit corridors, rooms, parking lots, and other areas

These factors should be considered in the assessment of violence within high-risk areas of the hospital.

NIOSH recommends preventive strategies that should be developed as part of a violence reduction program. These include the commitment of employees and senior management to reduce violent events, the identification of hazards within the workplace, safety and health training for all employees, and periodic evaluation of violence prevention programs.

NIOSH recommends general prevention strategies that require changes to the physical environment:

- Develop emergency signaling, alarms, and monitoring systems.
- Install security devices such as metal detectors to prevent armed persons from entering the hospital.
- Install other security devices, such as cameras and good lighting in hallways.
- Provide security escorts to the parking lots at night.
- Design waiting areas to accommodate and assist visitors and patients who may have a delay in service.
- Design the triage area and other public areas to minimize the risk of assault.
- Provide staff restrooms and emergency exits.
- Install enclosed nurses' stations.
- Install deep service counters or bullet-resistant and shatterproof glass enclosures in reception areas.
- Arrange furniture and other objects to minimize their use as weapons.

Administrative controls include:

- Design staffing patterns to prevent personnel from working alone and to minimize patient waiting time.
- Restrict the movement of the public in hospitals by card-controlled access.
- Develop a system for alerting security personnel when violence is threatened.
- Control access to staff working areas.
- Flag difficult patients.

Both OHSA and NIOSH indicate that the most significant and impactful reduction strategy is training. Training in de-escalation techniques and self-defense can help one better deal with difficult persons and protect employees from acts of violence. Training should also include a review of the hospital's policy on workplace violence so that staff know who to report incidents to and what measures to implement in the event of an incident.

Methods for the Reduction of Violence

There are many types of violence that occur within the healthcare setting. This includes violence from staff, patients, or visitors and violence that comes into the hospital from the outside, usually through the emergency department. Most healthcare organizations have policies and training that separately address each type of violent. However, combating violence is not about reacting to verbal abuse, assault, active shooters, bullying, domestic violence, or gang violence. Reducing violence is about preventing it before it occurs. Prevention protocols provide staff with tools that not only help them reduce the opportunity for violence but also make response more effective. Understanding the basic principles that cause violence enables staff to protect themselves, the hospital, and its occupants. Reducing the risk of violence within the hospital workplace is a comprehensive process that utilizes training and competency testing to proactively prepare staff to identify hazards before they occur. A violence reduction program must include a quick and organized response to the aftermath of violent events. Violent acts of any kind undermine an institution's culture, morale, and productivity. Effectively dealing with violent events after they occur reduces the long-term effects of the incident, allowing the hospital to flourish and staff to get back to work and feel safe again. Healthcare organizations must address violence within the organization as one entity, focusing on all types of violence together so that a comprehensive prevention process can be implemented.

Training

Hospitals must change what they train staff and how they train them. Training should focus on four aspects: customer service, de-escalation techniques, situational awareness, and response protocols. Training staff to understand the different types of violence and recognize potential violent situations provides them with tools to help resolve and/or react to violent situations better. The training process starts with customer service training for all hospital staff. A solid customer service program goes a long way in providing customer satisfaction and lowering stress for patients, visitors, and staff within the hospital, thus reducing the potential for violence. Many times, potentially violent situations start with a patient, visitor, or staff problem that escalates because staff do not know how to handle potentially difficult situations in a customer-focused way. Strong customer service promotes a caring and concerned environment that exemplifies staff attentiveness, dignity, respect, and more effective communication. Customer service provides a positive environment for all occupants within the healthcare environment, increasing customer satisfaction scores and reducing the potential for violent events.

Along with customer service training, all hospital staff should attend violence de-escalation training, learning techniques to help identify escalating violent behavior and interventions to de-escalate pending violent behaviors. Many times, hospital staff have to intervene when patients, visitors, or staff are already agitated and have reached their boiling point. Behavioral techniques that can de-escalate persons who are already agitated protect staff from violence and provide a more caring environment. Both customer service and de-escalation training programs should be refreshed annually, along with periodic and midterm competency reviews. Training updates should be part of staff meetings and huddles so that techniques are consistently reinforced. Security can play a major role in assisting staff in the training and review of these programs. Security staff should become trainers along with other department volunteers and work together to provide training and attend department meetings to conduct refresher training.

The next piece to violence prevention training is having staff in critical roles, a high-risk or security-sensitive area, learn situational awareness. Situational awareness training is new in the violence prevention arena but is a very important tool for staff to recognize potential threats not only when it comes to violence, but also in relation to other risk factors present within the healthcare environment. Situational awareness is a frame of mind in which you are aware of your surroundings and aware of whom or what could be of help to you if a problem were to arise. There are three major components to situational awareness:

1. Monitor normal activities or work patterns. Awareness of the normal operations of the day, people, activities, and objects allows for the determination of unusual or abnormal activities that may occur in the work area.
2. Trust your gut. Even though we may sense an abnormality within our work situation, we may ignore it because of our personal desire to avoid dangerous or confrontational situations. Awareness training allows staff to comfortably respond to adverse situations.
3. Avoid distractions. Distractions are situations that keep us focused on one event, blocking all other events that are occurring within the work environment, for example, when someone is texting while walking and runs into a fountain, robbing an individual of their situational awareness where it may be most needed.

Situational awareness training teaches staff to understand the different types of violence and recognize general threats before they occur. Staff learn to be more engaged at work and see patterns or trends in work routines as well as unusual events that could lead to violence or other safety issues.

Lastly, staff need to be trained in response protocols. This process should utilize an all-hazards approach. Staff should be trained to respond to violence like it is any disaster with standard procedures to follow. For example, active shooter response training should focus on how staff respond within their geographical location to the event. Like with fire response, staff should react differently depending on where they are in relation to the event. The response at a shooting location should be to run and hide. Adjacent areas should hide in place by closing all doors, as done in a fire response, or evacuate if patients are ambulatory. Reporting protocols for an actual event should be simple and consistent so that staff can react without having to look at a written policy. Again, like with any emergency, security or a designated department should be contacted in the event of any violent altercation.

Training of staff is only the beginning in providing a safer, violence-free environment. For the program to be effective, a solid reporting system should be put in place. Reporting should be simple and easy for staff to remember, and all types of violence should be reported the same way. Some hospitals use a general email address, like violence@acmehospital.org, to report violence issues like bullying or assault. The general email allows for privacy and ensures confidentiality. The reporting program should be penalty-free and not inadvertently penalize staff who are willing to report suspicious or unusual activity. Remember that reporting protocols should include all types of violence, like a hostile work environment.

The most difficult part of any violence prevention program is what to do with information when it has been reported. This is where most programs fail because poor handling of information causes staff to stop reporting out of fear of being singled out, fired, or not responded to. Incoming information should be triaged by a group composed of directors from several departments. This should include, but is not limited to, human resources, security, corporate compliance, risk management, operations, and nursing. All information should be considered confidential and further investigated by a representative from security and one from human resources, working together.

Policy

The last piece of a proactive violence reduction program is the creation and implementation of a violence reduction policy. The violence reduction policy should be constructed as an all-hazards approach addressing all types of violence and the hospital's response to violence. An all-hazards policy should include violence prevention measures that address:

- Staff-to-patient violence
- Patient-to-patient violence
- Staff-to-staff violence
- Severe injuries
- Active assailant
- Community mass casualty event

The plan should include procedures that address prevention, response, and recovery from a violent event, from a small verbal altercation to a full-scale physical assault. Procedures should include the response to both physical and psychological injuries for all persons involved. The policy should address the guidelines for arrest in the event of a workplace violence event. From a verbal altercation to a physical encounter, the handling of each type of event should be addressed specifically within the policy. There are no right or wrong answers when it comes to arrest or nonarrest; however, by having a policy in place, decisions can be more easily made when an event occurs.

Many professionals within the workplace violence space feel that a zero-tolerance policy is the best way to deter and handle a workplace violence incident. Many hospitals adopt a zero-tolerance policy so that they do not have to deal with the event, and fire or suspend all parties involved. This policy may not be the best fit for every hospital and should be evaluated before implementation. Experience has shown that eliminating both parties is not the best strategy, especially when it is clear to the staff who witnessed the event that the violence was one-sided. Removing both parties can make a tense situation worse within the department, lowering morale and forcing staff to take sides, potentially increasing the risk for future violent events. The best method is to have each situation investigated thoroughly to see where problems are occurring and to what extent before a final decision is made on the employment status of the event participants. For example, did a patient react because he or she was being inappropriately touched, or was the dispute between two employees because one was being bullied?

Media Relations

Media relations should also be part of the violence prevention and response policy. The hospital needs to be prepared to address any event, even when it is minor. A slow news day and an employee's social media post can change a situation dramatically. Public relations or any department that handles the media should be immediately informed of any violent event, so they are prepared to respond appropriately. The legal department or risk manager should also be informed immediately when an event occurs. Whether between staff or between patients or visitors, it is important for the legal department to know what is going on before they get a call from an outside attorney or police. The legal department should also be involved with the decision to arrest or not arrest a staff member, patient, or visitor.

Law Enforcement Response

As part of the violence prevention program, the police and emergency response teams should be part of the response protocols. The police should provide training to all hospital staff on their procedures related to violent incidents or active shooter. They should participate in drills and exercises and be invited into the facility at least once a year to tour it, so they are familiar with the hospital when they respond.[1]

Violence Prevention Drills

Conducting fire drills on a regular basis continually enforces the response process. Unit-specific drills help staff remember training and respond more effectively because training occurs within the staff's work environment. Drills pertaining to violent incidents like staff/patient assaults, domestic violence, or active shooters should be conducted within the work environment. Small mini-drills conducted within the work environment help staff feel more comfortable responding to violent situations, especially when training on active shooters. Unit-specific drills can make the difference between a quick, proper response and a panicked, disorganized reaction.

Difficult Patient Review Committee

Many hospitals have started to handle difficult patients by instituting a "difficult patient review committee." This committee comprises personnel from security, social work, human resources, risk management, physicians, and nursing. The committee's focus is the identification and review of difficult or violent patients and their care while in the hospital. Committee meetings occur on a regular basis or when an incident occurs. The committee reviews the patient's history along with violent events and develops a new care plan. When security, human resources, and clinical staff work together to review events that have occurred within the hospital, a plan can be developed to better care for the patient and protect staff, other patients, and visitors. Additionally, when staff see that difficult patients are being managed, they are more likely to report events and issues. Some examples of recommendations that could be made by this group include flagging difficult patients so that when they present, security can be notified in advance and be stationed on site or conduct frequent rounds by the treatment area while the patient is present. In some cases, it may be necessary to have security speak to the patient to ensure that they behave during a visit, outlining behavior expectations. When difficult patients present within clinics or the emergency department, staff can call security before an event occurs and security can again be present during that patient's visit.

Reference

1. Scaglione, Bernard J. and Anthony J. Luizzo. Aspects of crime and violence avoidance. *Journal of Healthcare Protection Management*, Vol. 33, No. 1, pp. 21–30, 2017.

Chapter 10

Information Security Management

Introduction

Of increasing importance to the healthcare security industry is network security. Risks to healthcare networks include stolen medical record information and loss of control to a hospital network held for ransom. To date, hundreds of thousands of medical records have been compromised to sell patient information, including credit card data, to the highest bidder. Over the past 10 years, several million records have been compromised. In 2015, the Office of Civil Rights (OCR) reported 253 healthcare breaches that affected 500 individuals or more with a combined loss of more than 112 million records. The data breaches accounted for just over 111 million records. Thirty-eight percent of the breaches were reported as unauthorized access by an employee. Close to 60% were reported as a hack from an outside source.[1] Hospitals hit with ransomware have lost control over their networks and lost access to their medical records. In 2016, of the malware attacks on the healthcare industry, 72% were caused by ransomware according to the Verizon 2017 Data Breach Investigations Report. The Verizon report found that ransomware attacks have doubled in frequency across all industries and are now the fifth most common malware. The healthcare industry was the second-most-targeted industry, at 15% of the overall incidents. Of the above-reported malware attacks in 2016, the healthcare industry was hit with 458 incidents, and 286 of these included improper data disclosure.[2]

Regulations and Guidelines

The Health Insurance Portability and Accountability Act of 1996 (HIPAA) and the Health Information Technology for Economic and Clinical Health Act (HITECH Act) are the information management security regulations specific to healthcare. HIPAA calls for the securing of medical information and HITECH for the reporting of it, as well as penalties assessed to hospitals for stolen medical information. Congress passed both the HIPAA and HITECH legislation to mandate all healthcare institutions to adoption federal privacy protection for individual's health information.

The Health Insurance Portability and Accountability Act was enacted in 1996 as Public Law 104-191 and published in the CFR under 45 CFR Parts 160, 162, and 164. HIPAA requires the Department of Health and Human Services (HHS) to adopt national standards for electronic healthcare transactions and code sets, unique health identifiers, and security. For medical record security, this included three primary rules: the Privacy Rule, Security Rule, and Enforcement Rule. HHS published the Privacy Rule in August 2002. This rule sets standards for the protection of individual health information for three types of covered entities: health plans, healthcare clearinghouses, and healthcare providers. Compliance with the Privacy Rule was required as of April 14, 2003. The Privacy Rule addresses the use and disclosure of individuals' health information or "protected health information." This rule sets the standards for individuals' privacy rights and control of how their health information is used. Within HHS, the Office for Civil Rights (OCR) has responsibility for implementing and enforcing the Privacy Rule with respect to voluntary compliance activities and civil money penalties. A major goal of the Privacy Rule is to ensure that individuals' health information is properly protected while allowing the flow of health information needed to provide and promote high-quality healthcare. The Security Rule was published in February 2003. This rule sets standards for protecting the confidentiality, integrity, and availability of electronic protected health information. Compliance with the Security Rule was required as of April 20, 2005. A major goal of the Security Rule is to protect the privacy of individuals' health information while allowing covered entities to adopt new technologies to improve the quality and efficiency of patient care. The Enforcement Rule provides standards for the enforcement of HIPAA rules. HHS enacted the Enforcement Rule through the Health Information Technology for Economic and Clinical Health Act. This rule imposes civil money penalties on entities that violate HIPAA rules.[3] The HITECH Act requires entities to notify patients of any unsecured data breaches related to protected health information (PHI). If a breach affects 500 or more patients, HHS must also be notified. Notification requirements are triggered whether the breach occurs internally or externally.

HIPAA requires all healthcare institutions to create and execute policies and procedures to meet the HIPAA requirements. These policies include:

- A general policy statement that summarizes the hospital's program and processes for the protection of PHI (see Appendix 1)
- The identification of a privacy and security officer to oversee the HIPAA program
- An outline of the training program given to staff so that they understand the HIPAA requirements
- The use and disclosure of protected health information
- The safeguarding of verbal and written protected health information
- The disclosure of to whom and when PHI is authorized for release
- Restrictions for the use of PHI
- The communication and access of PHI
- The accounting for disclosures of PHI
- The process for notification of a breach of unauthorized PHI
- The retention and destruction of PHI for both paper and electronic records
- Security for the maintenance of electronic PHI
- Physical security safeguards for all PHI
- The transportation and storage requirements for all PHI, including electronics[3]

ISO 27001

The International Organization for Standardization (ISO) was founded in 1947 as a worldwide federation of national standards bodies from some 100 countries, with one standards body representing each member country. The American National Standards Institute (ANSI) represents the United States. The name ISO is used around the world to denote the organization, thus avoiding the assortment of abbreviations that would result from the translation of "International Organization for Standardization" into the different national languages of its members. The ISO 27001 standard was published in October 2005, setting specific voluntary standards for an information security management system (ISMS). Although not specific to healthcare, the objective of the standard is to provide guidelines for establishing, implementing, maintaining, and continuously improving an ISMS. The standard outlines guidelines and general principles for initiating, implementing, maintaining, and improving information security management within an organization. The actual controls listed in the standard are intended to address the specific requirements identified through a formal risk assessment. The standard also provides a guide for the development of organizational security standards and effective security management practices. Organizations that meet the standard may be certified compliant by an independent and accredited certification body. Voluntarily, healthcare organizations can utilize and meet these standards as part of a solid network security program. Certification for ISO 27001 requires the following documentation:

- ISMS scope
- Information security policy
- Information security objectives
- Information risk assessment
- Information risk treatment
- Evidence of the competence of the people working in information security
- Other ISMS-related documents deemed necessary by the organization
- Operational planning and control documents
- Evidence of the monitoring and measurement of information security
- The ISMS internal audit program and the results of audits conducted
- Evidence of top management reviews of the ISMS

Additional voluntary standards include ISO 27004, which provides guidance on the development and use of measures and measurement for the assessment of an implemented information security management system as specified in ISO 27001. ISO 27005 covers information security risk management. The standard provides guidelines for information security risk management (ISRM) in an organization, specifically supporting the requirements of an information security management system defined by ISO 27001.[4]

Risks Associated with Electronic Information Management Security

People are the biggest risk to IT systems. Expired passwords, opening unauthorized emails, and not installing or upgrading software are the leading causes to unauthorized access into IT networks. Older computers, network switches, and routers that are no longer supported by the manufacturer for software upgrades and contain outdated software and virus protection can allow unauthorized backdoor access. Lack of software updates for current devices within the hospital network is another means of unauthorized access. This includes security devices like access control panels or servers and CCTV servers and IT cameras. Security departments and their integrators need to make sure that all security devices are up-to-date.

Employees are the number one threat to electronic information management. Generally, it is their lack of following policy that increases the risk of unauthorized access. Personal passwords are the number one cause to providing unauthorized access into hospital networks through PCs, laptop computers, or personal cell phone devices. Unauthorized access occurs when people create simple passwords, do not change passwords periodically, or share their passwords with other employees. Weak or simple passwords can give an outsider or another employee unauthorized access into the hospital network. Many people still use "1234" or other simple words or numbers as their password. Employees still feel comfortable sharing passwords between staff and departments for ease of use or frustration over complicated processes developed by IT departments.

Employees open emails or spam addressed to them by unknown persons. The opening of these foreign emails opens the door for external threats like viruses, malware, or ransomware.

Another high-risk group is vendors. Vendors are the second biggest threat to the hospital network. They may not see the need for security as the hospital does and not understand the importance of HIPAA regulations. Many times, vendor passwords are left within the hospital information management system. Like employees, their passwords may be simple so that they are easy to understand or transferable between workers. They may also leave a digital route in the system when conducting installation. Known as a "back door," many vendors leave remote access in place for repair, monitoring, or problem solving of the digital system. Leaving these unknown access points within the system provides an easy access path for unauthorized users.

Older network devices running within hospital networks present a formidable risk. These devices usually cannot be updated because they are no longer supported by the manufacturer. This includes PCs, routers, switches, cell phones, and any other device on the hospital network—security devices like CCTV cameras, access control panels, or CCTV servers. Software needs to be up-to-date as well. Software that is being utilized within the hospital may no longer be supported by the manufacturer or supported but not continually updated by vendors. All software patches and virus and malware protection should be up-to-date in order to minimize risks to the hospital network. Security software either on the hospital network or on a separate network with access into the hospital network needs to be constantly reviewed to ensure that all patches and protection are up-to-date. Maintenance contracts should include the updating of all software on all security network devices.

Keeping Your Network Secure

Ensuring that the hospital network is secure falls on the IT director and his or her staff. Strong processes and policies help in the reduction of risk to attack, but continued diligence works best. Users, whoever they are, need to be monitored to ensure that they are not under attack by an unauthorized person. Detecting a breach starts with the mapping of the hospital network. Mapping is the registration and cataloging of all network devices and specific information pertaining to the devices, like location, type, and age. This list or map can provide insight to the locations that present the highest risk to the network, knowing the network environment and where the important data resides. Inspect user profiles regularly to make sure they are authorized only in the areas they need for work. Audit the disposal of all network devices to ensure that they are disposed of properly. Software patches or upgrades in all devices or systems must be completed immediately when they become available. All systems and devices should have up-to-date software patches and virus protection.

Employees and Staff

■ Fix permissions to data to ensure only the right people have access.
■ Monitor exceptions and trends in user data.
■ Specify an index of approved software applications that are permitted and active on the network or device.
■ Ensure that patches are installed within the system and individual devices.
■ Install administrative privilege restrictions on all devices.

- Provide employee and vendor training on HIPAA policies and network security. Make sure that users understand the restrictions installed within the network and how these restrictions effect users' access and use within the system.
- Review user groups and access privileges on a regular basis and monitor users' rights.
- Create data owners. Data owners are employees given the responsibility to monitor access and systems to ensure that departmental or area staff are following network policies and security.
- Remove old data and devices from the system immediately when it is determined that they can no longer be patched or updated.
- Provide a screening process for all users wishing to access the hospital network. This should include the list of systems they are requesting access to and signed permission from department heads and/or vice presidents.
- Remove old users immediately upon their termination from employment or service. Some hospitals use a generic email address so that management can immediately request termination of access privileges when staff leave.
- Set standards for passwords. Employees and vendors should be required to use a variety of words, numbers, and symbols when creating passwords. Routine or periodic change of personnel passwords should be required.

Vendors and Contractors

- All vendors and contractors should be required to attend HIPAA and network security training.
- Password creation should be done for them and monitored to see if it is being used properly.
- Make sure passwords have a cutoff date and are removed from the system.
- Utilize business associate agreements. These are written contracts that outline network security policies and procedures and list penalties for noncompliance with them.
- Make sure that all hospital property is confiscated when vendors and contractors leave. This includes a search of their property to ensure that no hospital property is taken from the hospital.

Contingency Plan

It is extremely important to have contingency plans in place that address network outages, sabotage, or unauthorized access. Reacting as the event occurs creates lost hours of network availability and confidence in the IT department. Outages due to viruses or ransomware can lead to loss of medical record information and needed access to medical records for clinical staff treating patients.

Contingency planning starts with a risk assessment and evaluation of the network. Either internally or by a third party, the hospital network should be analyzed to determine physical access points, outdated software, and access permission violations. The assessment should also include remote electronic penetration testing to see if unauthorized access is possible. The risk assessment should be conducted at least annually, and recommendations should be implemented immediately upon notification.

Once the risk assessment is completed and vulnerabilities are determined, a response plan should be developed.

The response plan should address all types of potential exposures, including those determined by the risk assessment. This includes the discovery of a virus within the system, unauthorized access to medical or financial records, and the possibility of ransomware being downloaded into the hospital network. If a major attack should occur, it is best to get professional help immediately. Hospitals that have tried to resolve issues on their own have made situations worse and more difficult to repair by the time a professional is brought in. Have a third-party contract in place before an event occurs. This contract should include costs and response times. Having a contract in place prior to an event allows the hospital to choose the organization that best fits its needs and budget.[5]

References

1. Muni, Dan. Data breaches in healthcare totaled over 112 million records in 2015. *Forbes Magazine*, December 31, 2015. https://www.forbes.com/sites/danmunro/2015/12/31/data-breaches-in-healthcare-total-over-112-million-records-in-2015/#3fb009ba7b07.
2. Davis, Jessica. Ransomware accounts for 72% of healthcare malware attacks in 2016. *Healthcare IT News*, April 27, 2017. http://www.healthcareitnews.com/news/ransomware-accounted-72-healthcare-malware-attacks-2016.

3. Department of Health and Human Services. HIPAA for Professionals. Privacy Rule, Security Rule, Enforcement Rule. https://www.hhs.gov/hipaa/for-professionals/index.html.
4. The ISO Directory. An Introduction to ISO 27001, ISO 27002 … ISO 27008. http://www.27000.org/.
5. Department of Health and Human Services. *Security Standards: Administrative Safeguards. HIPAA Security Series*, Vol. 2, Paper 2, 3/2007. https://www.hhs.gov/sites/default/files/ocr/privacy/hipaa/administrative/securityrule/adminsafeguards.pdf?language=es.

Chapter 11

Evaluating Security Technology

Introduction

Technology changes at a rapid pace. The good news is that these changes help security departments do a better job. Costs of physical security applications have declined, and technology can be installed in places never thought possible in the past. What has changed is that technology has become digital. Digital technology has many distinct advantages. Digital signals can travel great distances for a minimal cost. Digital data can be presented in a variety of different ways, and digital data can be more readily collected and analyzed. When we say "digital technology" in the security field, we are talking about CCTV, card access, and alarm monitoring. The digital world allows all security devices to communicate together, providing an integrated approach. For example, a door contact alarm point can communicate with an access control device and/ or CCTV camera mounted close by. In addition, digital security applications can interface with digital mapping, GPS, Wi-Fi, or smartphones and tablets.

Physical security applications are now Internet Protocol (IP) enabled, making the evaluation and purchase of physical security applications more complicated. Digital technology has some real advantages over the conventional tube and solid-state security systems utilized in the late 1990s. Understanding how digital technology works and its limitations is important in the specification and purchase of IP-based digital security systems. Making the right choice is important since oftentimes security funds are limited, and the purchase of ineffective systems can lead to embarrassment for the security director who purchases them. Because of the complicated nature of IP-based systems, security professionals are turning to vendors and hospital IT departments to make decisions on the specification and purchase of new systems. Before new systems and applications are chosen, every security director should have some basic knowledge of how IP-based security systems and their components work so that an educated decision can be made that provides for the best applications and systems for the hospital.

The field of digital security technology refers to CCTV, card access, personnel identification, and alarm monitoring applications. Once these applications are converted to a digital format, they can work together to provide a converged, single integrated application—hence the term "convergence." The digital world allows all security devices to communicate collectively, providing a truly integrated system. In addition to security devices, digital security applications can interface with digital mapping, GPS, or Wi-Fi in order to collect, organize, and distribute information. Digital security can interface with different databases, which can provide information like photos, street addresses, fingerprints, and any other information an end user may require. All of this information can be integrated into one single distributed database that can be presented on a single or multiple PCs, tablets, or smartphones.

Advantages to Digital Security Technology

Digital security technology has many distinct advantages over the old analog type utilized years ago. First, digital data can travel great distances without signal degradation and loss of quality. During new construction digital technology can be installed for a third of the cost of conventional security systems, digital data can be distributed and presented in a variety of different formats, digital data can be stored with a minimum of space and cost, and digital data can be retrieved quickly and efficiently.

IP security technology utilizes fiber-optic cable to transmit security signals and data. In conjunction with CAT cable, these two forms of transmission medium are the most effective and cheapest way to connect security devices and provide a distributed network for monitoring and responding to security-related situations. The cost of installing cable connections for all IP security devices is negligible. Security devices run on the same cable as phone and computer systems. Phone and computer cables are automatically included in construction and renovation costs and are rarely removed as a cost-cutting measure as security systems have been in the past. Even conversion costs for upgraded security systems are low since fiber-optic cable exists within the hospital structure already. Once a security system is set up within the hospital, network video, alarm, and access control data can be distributed to any computer within the hospital for monitoring or display; there is no need for special computers or computer devices to display security software. Data can be placed on the hospital network so that it can be accessed from remote locations or through the Internet.

Understanding How Digital Security Systems Work

Understanding how digital systems work and the best use of these systems starts with the understanding of the key components that make up the foundation for digital security systems. It is important to understand how digital technology works and what limitations and benefits devices and systems have before purchasing and installing them.

How a Network Operates

The most significant element of the digital world is the "network." A network carries the digital signals between devices utilized in physical security applications. By definition, a digital network or Ethernet is a series of computers or devices wired together in order to exchange information within the group of devices; it is also refer to as a local area network (LAN) or wide area network (WAN). A LAN is a network of several devices linked together in an immediate area, usually in the same building or on one floor of a building. A WAN is a network of computers or devices that cover a building or campus. It refers to a multibuilding or multisite configurations connected together. A typical IP security layout is shown in Figure 11.1.

All networks are set up with a set of rules or a "protocol" that provides standardized communication between computers. The rules are guidelines that regulate how data is transferred from one computer to another. Typically, networks utilize an Internet Protocol/Transport Control Protocol (IP/TCP) configuration. This type of configuration is the most commonly utilized protocol and is a packet-switch network configuration. This means that data is transmitted in two packets of data. One packet is the information being sent. The second packet is the network protocol; it describes how the information is received and understood by the receiving computer.

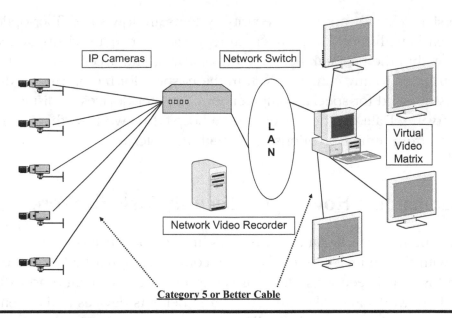

Figure 11.1   A typical security CCTV IP network configuration.

Network Bandwidth

The key to a successful installation of a digital security system is the network—ensuring that the network has the bandwidth capacity necessary to operate the devices and products purchased for the security application. Also important is making sure that the network has room to grow so future devices can be installed and work correctly within the guidelines of the network. There are specific aspects of a network that are important to understand when deciding to use security systems in a network configuration. Bandwidth is the most important aspect to consider for security applications. Bandwidth refers to how much data can be sent through a transmission medium or wire. When you refer to bandwidth, or bit rate, you are referring to bits of data transmitted every second through a transmission medium. This is referred to as bits per second (bps). As an example, a full page of English text is about 16,000 bits of data; a fast modem can move data at about 57,000 bps. Full-motion/full-screen video requires a bandwidth of 10,000,000 bps. Bandwidth or bit rate capacity depends on the size of the physical wire and the devices the wires are connected to. To understand the concept of bandwidth, think of a wastewater drain pipe system. The pipe diameter (bandwidth) can support only so many sinks, toilets, and other devices to effectively drain waste. In the design of the waste system, the drain pipe must be wide enough to allow drainage when all of the devices are at full capacity and working simultaneously. If designed incorrectly, the drain will back up or stop draining. In the case of a digital network, overload can cause devices to slow down, shut off, or reduce their bandwidth, causing signal degradation and/or data loss.

Switches and Routers

The wires that come out of the back of each computer or network device are connected to a switch. Switches enable the communication between multiple computers, printers, or security devices within the network. A switch organizes and distributes data packets from the networked devices and transmits them throughout the LAN or WAN. Switches vary in size, from four ports and up. Switches can also be connected to additional switches to increase the capacity of the network. A switch cannot access the Internet or other LANs; this requires a device called a router. A switch connects to a router, and a router selectively transmits data according to an IP address to another computer, switch, or other router. In order for data to be transferred from computer to computer and switch to switch, there needs to be a physical cable connected to each that will transfer the data packets from place to place.

Transmission Mediums

There are six categories of transmission medium that are utilized in a network configuration: coaxial cable, twisted-pair cable, unshielded twisted-pair (UTP), shielded twisted-pair, category program cable (CAT cable), and fiber-optic cable. The most frequently utilized wiring types are coaxial cable, twisted-pair cable, UTP, CAT cable, and fiber-optic cable. Coaxial cable is a copper-based cable type that can support up to 100 Mbps of data. It is fairly inexpensive, and cable can be run up to 500 meters before a signal boost is required. Twisted-pair cable can be used to transmit digital data. Twisted-pair is a pair of wires twisted together to form a circuit that transmits data. Twisted-pair cabling is made from copper wires. There are two basic types: shielded twisted-pair and unshielded twisted-pair. UTP is the least expensive of all wire types. It is the fastest copper-based medium and requires signal boosts every 100 meters. UTP is used in most networking architectures. Today's UTP is referred to as category program cable. CAT cable usually has a numerical designation that refers to the transmission capacity or production generation. The current standard for CAT cable is CAT 7, which can support up to 10 Gbps, transmitting up to 100 Gb at 600 Mhz.

Fiber-optic cabling supports transmission speeds of more than 1 Gbps (gigabits per second), making it the fastest cabling choice. It can also be run for longer distances than UTP. It can transmit 40 miles with off-the-shelf equipment. UTP and coaxial cabling use copper wire, which is susceptible to electrical interference. Fiber-optic works differently by converting data (bits) into beams of light, which do not carry electrical impulses. Fiber-optic cabling is the most often used cable, alongside cheaper CAT cable to create a backbone of a network (drain pipe). Fiber can be used for both analog and digital transmissions. The best configuration for a security network is a fiber backbone with CAT cables connecting each device. Fiber is used to connect all of the switches and routers together. CAT 6 or 7 cables are used to connect each device to the switch. The fiber provides the largest-diameter pipe or transmission capacity. CAT 6 or 7 is a smaller and cheaper pipe, just large enough to support the flow of data for any single device into the main drain pipe.

If an existing network is going to be used for the security system, the transmission medium should be investigated. Older networks may be running CAT 4 or 5 cable with little or no fiber. Remember that the program category cable number defines the bandwidth, and if it's an older installation it may be too restrictive to work on newer security devices, or the security device may need to reduce the quality of the signal it transmits so that it can transmit on a smaller pipe. Too small a pipe may also delay alarm signals or dramatically reduce the quality of video. Even CAT 6 or 7 cables utilized without a fiber backbone can restrict the bandwidth of some IP security devices.

Network Configurations

The first hurdle to overcome when committing to networked security systems is deciding between developing a new, separate network and using the existing hospital network. The major stumbling block associated with a separate network configuration is the cost of the installation. However, several strands of fiber are all that is necessary to transmit the signals from multiple cameras and alarm points. The use of a separate or independent network for security systems is usually not a problem for most modern network setups.

Today, fiber with high-volume CAT cables dominates most hospital network systems. However, when deciding to use the hospital network for the collection and distribution of video, the hospital IT department should be part of the decision and be able to meet with the video manufacturer to discuss network capabilities and use for both the hospital systems and the security systems. Consideration should also be given when installing some of the new high-resolution cameras, high-definition (HD) or 4K. The newer cameras can utilize a high rate of bandwidth, and as IP cameras increase in resolution, their bandwidth may become greater. Large bandwidth is also necessary when analytics are going to be used since video compression does not work effectively with many analytics.

Before finalizing the decision to create a new network or use an existing one, two other issues need to be considered: network redundancy and network reliability. If you are going to utilize a new network, then redundancies should be built in so that communication can continue if the network should fail. Redundancies include building a "SONET ring" network configuration with network servers attached remotely to local switches. Figure 11.2 demonstrates a typical SONET ring fiber-optic configuration.

When utilizing an existing hospital network, research should be done on its downtime history and reliability. If the existing network is not reliable and has large periods of downtime, then the security system may be unreliable as well. Again, some of the downtime can be eliminated by installing network servers at the local switch and ensuring that all switches and

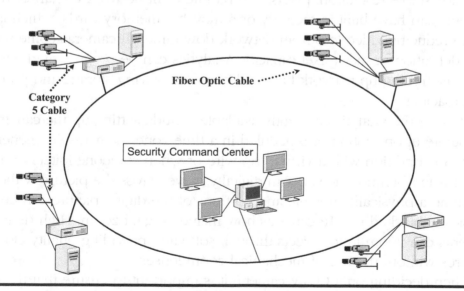

Figure 11.2 Typical SONET ring configuration.

servers are plugged into emergency power. In addition, most IP cameras have built-in memory that will store video when the network goes offline and then transmit video when the network comes back online. It is important when purchasing cameras to ensure that they have a reasonable amount of data storage or storage that is compatible with the average network downtime.

When assessing the idea of constructing a separate security network, consideration should be given to constructing the network through renovation projects or during new construction. Because of the low cost of wiring, a hospital renovation project or major construction project can add to the creation and completion of a fiber backbone for security. Then security devices can be connected to the network slowly as budgets allows.

Internet Protocol Cameras

Besides providing a digital platform, Internet Protocol (IP) cameras offer some real advantages over analog cameras. IP cameras can be wireless, and PTZ (pan-tilt-zoom) can be controlled over the network, requiring less cabling. IP cameras can be powered over the network utilizing one cable for both power and video signal. IP camera systems are scalable and flexible and allow for open architecture. IP camera video is easily transferable to hard drives, so searching and retrieving video is faster and easier. They have adjustable resolution, pixels, and bit rate to fit network demands. IP cameras can have built-in memory or removable memory cards, which is key to reducing video loss from network downtime. IP cameras come with high-definition or megapixel capacity. Analytics can be programmed into cameras, freeing up network bandwidth and improving storage and processing capacities.

Some of the analytics currently available include setting up the camera to operate upon motion or scheduled in a time zone. Cameras can generate an alarm condition with a virtual trip wire or when someone loiters or an object is left behind. Viewers can digitally move across the picture without the camera physically moving, and portions of the digital picture can be physically blacked out. IP cameras now include digital zoom. High-definition cameras can zoom in to objects through software, providing quality close-up pictures without the use of mechanical zoom lenses.

When deciding on a CCTV camera, it is important to ensure that the camera software is compatible with the video management software purchased.

Many times, the wrong camera is installed and the video quality or operation of the camera can be poor, leaving a camera useless in the protection of patients, visitors, and staff. Conversations with the camera vendor, the video management vendor, and the hospital IT department can help to determine the cameras that best fit the security system and provide the best-quality picture and analytics.

Internet Protocol Video Recorders

When assessing a video recording system, several features need to be reviewed before purchasing and utilizing digital recorders. There are two types of digital recorders on the market today: digital video recorders (DVRs) and network video recorder (NVRs). DVRs were developed to replace video tape recorders, and they convert analog video into digital video and then compress the video for storage. When retrieved from storage, the video is uncompressed and converted back to an analog video signal. Current DVRs can record both analog and digital cameras. When converting analog video to digital and back again, there will be loss of picture quality; that is why NVRs are the preferred recorder technology. However, in order to obtain the full benefits of NVRs, it is best to be completely digital, utilizing IP cameras connected to a network. Both units can be remotely located in the field and networked back to a command center or any PC for reviewing or recording.

DVRs are produced to input a specified number of cameras and record a specified or fixed number of frames per second. The more cameras used in each box, the less frames per second per camera that are available for recording. For example, if a recording box can record a total of 200 fps and is equipped to handle 20 camera inputs, when 20 cameras are installed, each camera can only record up to 10 fps. If fewer cameras are used in each box, then the recording rate will increase. For example, if 10 cameras are plugged into the recording box, then each camera can record up to a maximum of 20 fps.

Storage capacity is also a consideration when evaluating a DVR or NVR. A recording unit will contain a single, large-volume hard drive to store video data. Some units come equipped with backup internal hard drives; others use a drive array as built-in redundancy in the event that the main drive fails. The array records video one drive at a time. If a drive fails, the system will automatically transfer recording to the next drive in the array. The bad drive can be quickly replaced so that the system can continue to record at capacity. When selecting a recording system, make sure the hard drive is large enough to store all of the cameras for the time frame requested. Recording time is based on the number of cameras, camera pixels, movement in the field of view of each camera, and amount of pan, tilt, and zoom used by the camera operator.

The last item to consider is the system's networkability. Can recording boxes be combined so that they can be viewed together on one software program? In order to simultaneously view video images from different boxes, the video recording software should interconnect all of the cameras and recording boxes so that they all can be seen and/or be retrieved from any location or PC. Viewing software should also be evaluated when purchasing a recorder. Some systems need to connect directly to each recording box and can only be viewed with vendor-specific software. Other systems are web based and only require a web browser to view and retrieve stored video from the recording system.

Assessing Digital Compression Technology

When assessing the viability of an IP camera or video recorder, compression technology, image presentation technology, and frame rate should be evaluated before purchasing. These three aspects of the digital products determine the bandwidth utilized and the quality of the image that is either recorded or presented on a monitor. When deciding to use IP cameras, along with digital video recorders or network recorders, it is important to understand video compression. In order to send a video signal effectively across a network, the video file size must be reduced, similar to the idea of "zipping" a file so that you can send it in an email. Compressing streaming video data is necessary in order to ensure that the network is not overwhelmed by large amounts of data being sent through the network at the same time. If the video is not compressed, a network could easily shut down or crash due to an overflow of digital traffic.

Video compression is used to transmit streaming video from a camera to a monitor or recorder. Recorders compress video as well, in order to increase video storage capacity. The higher the compression ratio, the smaller the amount of bandwidth that is used; however, the higher the degradation of the image once uncompressed for viewing.

Video can be transmitted or stored as either full frame or conditional storage. Conditional storage is known as either lossless or lossy compression.

Lossless compression means that the original data is reconstructed exactly as it was before it was compressed. Lossy compression means that certain data is lost during the conversion. The loss occurs mostly in the picture resolution. Compressing video can cause reduced color nuances and reduced color resolution; it can remove small, invisible parts of the picture and may not record parts of the picture that don't change as the picture sequences.

One of the most common forms of compression technology is called JPEG or M-JPEG, which stands for Joint Photographic Experts Group or Motion Joint Photographic Experts Group. JPEG compression technology records every video frame and compresses each frame by combining pixels into large blocks that are transported over the network and then reconstructed when the video is displayed. JPEG can reduce file size to about 5% of its normal size. High Efficiency Video Coding (HEVC), or H.265, is the newest compression technology, designed for megapixel cameras. This standard provides as much as 50% or more of compressed video compared with its predecessor, H.264. H.265 was developed by the Joint Collaborative Team on Video Coding (JCT-VC), an organization that brings together image and video encoding experts from around the world.

Another aspect of compression technology is the picture presentation. When retrieving video from a recorder or directly from an IP camera, the size of the video picture that appears on the computer screen is called Common Intermediate Format (CIF). CIF appears in four formats or sizes, CIF through 4 CIF. CIF, or 1 CIF, presents a picture about the size of a Post-it note, 4 inches long by 3 inches high. 4 CIF, the largest format, is the size of a full computer screen. The smaller the CIF, the less disk space or bandwidth that is utilized. The problem with 1, 2, or 3 CIF presentation is that the picture becomes blurry and distorted when it is blown up to a 4 CIF size.

The next consideration is frames per second (fps). This refers to how many video frames are sent per second from the camera or are recorded on the recorder's hard drive. In the videotape world, a typical security installation recorded 3–7.5 fps. In order to compare digital technologies, a TV picture transmits at 30 fps and the human eye perceives full motion at 16 fps.

Again, the lower the frame rate, the less bandwidth and the less disk space that is utilized. When it comes to compression technology, frames per second, and CIF presentation, the best way to assess what works for your particular needs is to see different applications in an actual field setting. There are several different compression technologies on the market, each compressing and uncompressing video differently. When accessing a system, remember that a low compression rate in a 4 CIF format at 30 fps produces a very high-quality video image but will require a high amount of bandwidth.

Security Equipment Standardization

The security departments should look to develop standards in CCTV, door locks, access control locks, door hardware, and software applications. The creation and implementation of standards in technology is important. It provides:

- Ease of installation and repair
- Familiarity of devices
- Ease of operation
- Simplification in purchasing

These standards should include specific manufacturers and models that should be installed for access control, alarm monitoring, and CCTV cameras. The current security integrators can help set up the standards, and all components should be purchased through the integrator, not the IT department. The security department should meet with their security integrators and decide what types of equipment will be used at the hospital. CCTV cameras, door contacts, motion detectors, and panic buttons should all be specified by the specific manufacturer, make, and model. Then a standard request for proposal (RFP) can be developed so that any integrator can read and understand what products should be specified in the proposal. Once specific products are chosen, the design and layout should be specified. Drawings/ schematics should be developed to use with an RFP that show what equipment should be used and how to support the security device that will be installed. Today, since security equipment is low voltage and uses network cable to transmit its signal, security equipment is installed in IT closets or low-voltage closets. Security equipment like controllers, lock power supplies, and CCTV camera recorders should all be installed in IT closets utilizing rack-mounted equipment, when possible. Standard drawings/schematics should also show the power and space requirements necessary for a standard installation.

CCTV cameras and video storage devices have their own special requirements. But again, these products should be standardized. The main reason for doing so is ease of use for the hospital staff. When new equipment is installed, the hospital staff will know how to use it right away. In addition to using the same manufacturer, standards should be developed stating the type of CCTV camera models used and the picture quality, like the use of dome or ceiling-mounted cameras. In areas like behavioral health or the emergency department, these domes should be vandal-proof. In the infant and children areas, HD cameras should be considered so that the best possible image can be captured in the event of a domestic dispute or child kidnapping.

System and Procedural Failure

Failure rates refer to equipment that has stopped operating or works intermittently. Ensuring that digital security systems function 100% of the time is important to the security function; when those systems fail, temporary processes should immediately be put in place that provide the same level of security as the original systems. Every security department should monitor equipment failure rates. When a camera stops working, or an alarm contact is torn off of a door, the level of security is diminished. Most important is the process of maintaining the same level of security until a repair is completed, which makes failure rate monitoring so important. Systems or processes should be put in place in advance to identify failures of equipment immediately and to invoke temporary measures that will provide the same or close to the same level of security until the equipment can be repaired.

Most electronic access control systems are supervised and monitor all of the devices wired into them real time. When a door contact or motion sensor goes bad or is broken, an alarm is generated. In addition, most systems have an area that can be accessed within the software to see all of the device's status, or a report can be generated listing any alarms or device status. In addition to digital checks, periodic physical checks of devices must be done. Device checks should be visual inspections conducted at a frequency equal to their importance—panic buttons more frequently than door contacts, etc. In addition, alarm devices should be given maintenance on a regular basis to again ensure that they are working properly and to extend their useful life. The regular inspection of security equipment is important to ensure that it is working as designed. For example, many hospitals conduct monthly checks of the physical security applications in the maternity and pediatric areas to ensure that the level of security installed works as designed. For maternity and pediatrics, it is checking the infant tags to make sure they are operational—actually bringing a tag to the door to see if it locks and/or the alarm sounds, checking all doors that have magnetic locks installed in order to make sure that magnetic locks engage properly and the doors close correctly. Video from the CCTV cameras is checked to make sure they are recording and that the recorded video meets the standards of installation. The same could be said for panic buttons and card readers. Panic buttons should be checked regularly to make sure they are working correctly. Many times, a staff member will hit the button in an emergency and find out then that it is not working because it was not reset after an accidental unnoticed push. Card reader doors should be checked to see if they are locking. Sometimes these doors may not be operational, and no one knows because they routinely present their card to the reader and open the door. Rarely does staff try a door to make sure it is locked before presenting their access card.

What happens when a device fails? First, the loss of a device or system must be identified immediately because in most cases the level of security drops or is nonexistent. Once notification has been made, a temporary system should be instituted. This plan may include posting a security officer or staff member in the area, shutting down the area, or changing procedures until devices can be repaired. Either way, a predetermined plan must be established that will address any and all failures of physical security devices, and these plans need to be reviewed and tested at least yearly.

Downtime plans need to be tested periodically to ensure that procedures work effectively. Drills or tabletop exercises should be conducted at least annually. Drill critiques should be conducted, and the results of the drill documented, including any resolutions for change to procedures on all areas identified during the exercise. Downtime procedures should then be modified to meet the recommended changes as determined by the drill or tabletop exercise.[1]

Reference

1. Scaglione, Bernard J. Digital security technology simplified. *Journal of Healthcare Protection Management*, Vol. 23, No. 2, pp. 51–60, 2007.

Chapter 12

The Security Survey

Introduction

In healthcare, the assessment of risk is very important. Identifying risks to patients, visitors, and staff is paramount in providing quality care and maintaining a safe environment for all occupants. One way to assess and mitigate risk is through the use of a security survey. The security survey is a thorough examination of the hospital's security practices and its operations to evaluate facility risk and liabilities. Security surveys should be completed annually within high-risk or security-sensitive areas, with a thorough evaluation of the entire facility once every three years. Security surveys should result in improvements to the overall security program and reduce facility risk. The goal of any security survey is to find risks within the security of the hospital and then determine recommendations to mitigate the identified risks. Recommendations are then implemented and tracked to ensure that identified risks are mitigated.

Guidelines and Standards for the Assessment of Risk

Several healthcare organizations now publish guidelines and standards specific to the assessment of risk that can assist security in undertaking a security survey. The Joint Commission (TJC) has a standard for a healthcare security survey. The standard states: "The hospital manages safety and security risks. The hospital identifies safety and security risks associated with the environment of care (EOC) noting risks are identified from:

■ Internal sources such as ongoing monitoring of the environment
■ Results of root cause analyses
■ Results of annual proactive risk assessments of high-risk processes
■ Credible external sources such as 'Sentinel Event Alerts'"

In addition, the Joint Commission issued Sentinel Event Alert Number 45 on June 3, 2010, entitled "Preventing Violence in the Healthcare Setting." It requires all healthcare institutions to:

■ Identify strengths and weaknesses and make improvements to the facility's violence prevention program
■ Take extra security precautions in the emergency department, especially if the facility is in an area with a high crime rate or gang activity

The International Association for Healthcare Security and Safety (IAHSS) has published guidelines for security risk assessments, which suggest that healthcare facilities identify vulnerable assets and threats to those assets, and develop risk mitigation strategies to protect those assets. It also has a healthcare-specific risk assessment model to help healthcare organizations identify and mitigate risks. These documents are available through membership in the organization.

ASIS International has published a document entitled "Standard (RA): Risk Assessment." This document provides direction on developing and conducting an effective risk assessment program, including principles, managing a risk assessment program, performing individual risk assessments, and providing competencies of risk assessors. This document is available at the ASIS International bookstore or for free if you are a member of the organization.

Aspects of the Security Survey

The security survey is a tool that is important in the mitigation of risk. It helps in the reduction of risk by identifying potential threats and vulnerabilities. A complete and thorough security survey identifies assets to be protected, determines threats and vulnerabilities, pinpoints areas for improvement, and helps in the development of recommendations to reduce risk. The survey should be an analysis of security features in place, analyzing entry points, security staffing levels, physical security systems, and policies and procedures specific to the security of staff, visitors, and patients residing within the hospital. It should look for security deficiencies like broken locks, lights out, valuables that are left unattended, and visitors who leave personal property unattended in waiting or patient rooms. Security surveys can be conducted facility-wide, within identified high-risk areas, or even within identified hot spot areas determined through incident data analysis. For example, if incidents within the hot spot area are thefts, the survey tool should focus on demographics related to the theft, i.e., type of property taken, entry point to obtain the property, time of day, and day of the week.

The security survey starts as a walk-through of the hospital buildings and property. It should be consistent with general security practices, working from the property line and moving inward toward the buildings, and then surveying the interior of the buildings focusing on high-risk areas. As Figure 12.1 demonstrates, the security survey process is undertaken through the analysis of concentric circles.

The survey process starts at the hospital property line. Evaluate any property designations like fencing, lighting, or greenery. Ensure that the property line physical barriers are secure: no holes in fencing, broken

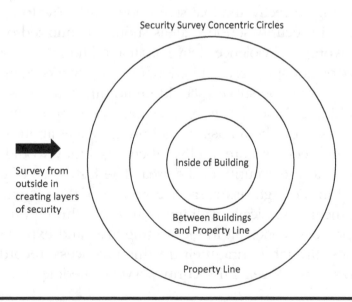

Figure 12.1   Security survey concentric circles.

gates, or large gaps between fencing and gates. Ensure that lighting is adequate and the greenery trimmed so that a perpetrator does not have a place to hide or can utilize trees to climb over fencing. The next phase is to survey between the property line and the hospital buildings. This includes parking lots, storage buildings, and roadways. Again, lighting needs to be assessed along with greenery. Make sure that shrubs are no higher than three feet and tree limbs do not block lighting on poles or attached to buildings. This part of the survey also includes CCTV coverage, ensuring that the camera does what it is intended to do, viewing the places desired by security, with effective operation during the night and day (from sun glare). The next phase of the survey is a walk-through of the exterior of all hospital buildings. Check doors, windows, and all other entry and exit points. Ensure that all doors and windows that are supposed to be locked are locked and that all unlocked entrances are working as required. Doors should be locked and unlocked during the times designated by the hospital.

The last phase of the security survey is a review of the inside of the hospital buildings. This includes a complete walk-through of the entire hospital and other buildings, starting at the roof and ending in the basement. The focus of the survey should be on general security practices like locked doors and other installed physical security measures to ensure that they are working correctly. During this part of the survey, security-sensitive areas should be given a thorough walk-through to ensure that all security measures are in place and working correctly and that staff understand how to operate them. In addition, staff in security-sensitive areas should be quizzed on security protocols like workplace violence, active assailant, and infant abduction.

In high-risk or hot spot areas, additional survey work should be completed. A security opinion survey should be administered to staff, patients, and visitors utilizing a specific set of questions focusing on their security and safety. This survey should ask users how they feel about security, what makes them feel insecure, and what changes they would recommend for improvement to the security of the area. The last piece of the security survey within the high-risk areas is a review of the patient and visitor process. That means physically walking from entry through treatment to see how the process works. Sit in the waiting area and experience what the patient goes through during their treatment process, recording the step-by-step process. (A general security survey schedule can be found in Appendix 2.)

Recommendation Process

Data gathered through the security survey, the opinion survey, and the patient flow analysis, along with incident and call for service data, should be reviewed in detail. Security defects that were identified during the survey should be grouped along with common themes identified within the other data gathered: survey results, patient flow analysis, and incident data. Themed or grouped data should be reviewed based on the frequency of similar results. These themed results will provide the data that will focus the evaluation on solutions that will be successful in the reduction of risk throughout the facility and in the identified security-sensitive areas.

Recommendations to correct or reduce the risks or defects found during the survey process are developed out of the information evaluation process. This process should be conducted by the security survey team. The security department should develop a team that will conduct the survey, record findings, and review findings to help in the development of recommendations. Members of the evaluation team should include security department personnel that have training or experience in conducting security surveys. These include a security supervisor or manager, a locksmith, a physical security specialist, an investigator, and management personnel from the identified security-sensitive areas. The team leader of this group should be the person on the team that has the most experience conducting security surveys. Once the security team completes the survey, they should sit down and evaluate the data, grouping similar defects or findings together so that recommendations can be developed.

The resulting data should be reviewed by another team. A group of hospital staff can help in identifying recommendations and their implementation. Utilizing a team provides buy-in for recommendations, making them part of the security process. The role of the team is to review the recommendations and determine which are the most feasible to implement based on funding availability. Many hospitals utilize their EOC security committee or security committee to accomplish this task. If a security committee does not exist, then one should be created. Team members should include security, nursing, administration, facilities, and department heads from identified high-risk areas. The team's goal is to review the survey data and recommendations and develop a strategy to implement recommendations. The team will then track the implemented recommendations to ensure that they are working effectively in the reduction of risk.

Recommendation Implementation and Tracking

Once recommendations are narrowed down, the key to true risk mitigation is the completed implementation of recommendations developed from the survey process and the tracking of their effectiveness. Recommendations should be tracked in order to ensure that they are implemented by the hospital. A tracking form should be produced that summarizes recommendations, estimates cost, assigns responsibility, and sets implementation dates. Recommendation implementation should be part of the security report submitted to administration for regulatory compliance. Figure 12.2 provides a sample of a tracking tool that can help to effectively track all recommendations until implemented.

The tracking tool can be used to monitor each recommendation until it is implemented. Recommendations developed from the security survey may not always be implemented by the hospital. Some recommendations may be too expensive to implement, require major changes to the physical plant or equipment, or be too expensive to purchase given the hospital budget. Additionally, some recommendations may just be turned down by hospital administration not wishing to provide that level of security for patients,

HOSPITAL NAME						
SURVEY NAME						
DATE						
Tracking Number	Survey Recommendation	Response to Recommendation	Implementation Plan	Priority	Cost Estimate	Person Responsible
	Priority—Security Financial Ability to Implement					

Figure 12.2   Recommendation tracking form.

visitors, and staff. When this situation arises, a survey recommendation cannot just be dropped from the tracking tool. The team must reevaluate the recommendation and either find an alternative resolution or document the reason for noncompliance. Noncompliant documentation cannot just indicate the inability to fund the recommendation. A more systematic reason must be given, like an alternative recommendation or the rationale that the hospital has established the level of security that it feels is adequate for the protection of patients, visitors, and staff. This documentation should include data that will help in the reasoning for the change in the recommendation. For example, a recommendation may be made to provide visitor passes or to lock the doors to a given treatment area. Hospital administration may not want any restrictions for visitors and just say no to passes or locked units. In this case, an alternative should be made, like passes issued only at night or frequent patrols through a treatment area. If it is decided that even the alternate recommendation will not be implemented, then a statement on the general security within the hospital may be sufficient to reduce liability related to the survey recommendation. A statement outlining the hospital's philosophy on free access to patients and visitors may be enough.

Once a recommendation is implemented, the job of the evaluation team is not over. All agreed-upon recommendations should be tracked past implementation to ensure that they are effective in the mitigation of risk. Ensuring that the recommended remedies work is the last part of the assessment process. Before a recommendation is implemented, an improvement process should be developed. The purpose of the process is to collect information that will help in the determination of the recommendation's success. Answer this question: Is the implemented recommendation effective in mitigating the risk identified during the survey process? The tracking process can include the collection of incident data, a periodic staff opinion survey, or even a resurvey during an identified time period, like three or six months. The evaluation team should monitor the effectiveness of all implemented recommendations over a one-year period or longer to ensure that the recommendation is actually reducing the identified risk.

A Metrics-Based Model for Risk Assessment

Conducting a security risk assessment is essential to providing more effective security services. The results of a well-conducted security risk assessment provide valuable information that can be incorporated into everyday operations and serve as a roadmap toward more efficient security services and continuous process improvement. In all aspects of the evaluation, metrics should be used to justify each component of the security program. A metrics-based assessment provides a nonbiased survey, focusing on identifying avenues to improve the capabilities of security services.

Metrics-based assessments utilize data to determine high-risk areas and risk probabilities. Unlike traditional assessments, which rely on physically surveying the hospital to pinpoint inadequacies within the current security program, metrics-based analysis highlights data to illustrate avenues for improvement. A metrics-based assessment provides the security director with a view of the immediate and tactical concerns as well as a strategic perspective to help mitigate risk in the future.

A metrics-based assessment starts with the determination of high-risk or security-sensitive areas. This data is obtained through analysis of:

- Incident data review
- Benchmarking with like hospitals
- Literature review of organizational publications
- Calls for service data
- Complaint data
- Staff and patient survey data
- Self-reporting survey data
- Industry standards and guidelines

Once analyzed, the data will yield categories to be developed that identify specific areas for improvement. Then those high-risk or security-sensitive areas can be surveyed and assessed to determine what methods for improvement will be most effective.

For example, incident and call for service data can be broken down by incident demographics, i.e., time of day, incident type, day of the week, and victim type. Benchmark data that identifies problems other hospitals may be experiencing. Another source of data important to the assessment includes self-reporting surveys. Surveys should be developed specifically for each high-risk area and administered to staff, patients, and visitors. Questions should request general information on the security of the area, like how safe they feel, or do they have security concerns? Then more specific questions can be asked that relate to the data collected identifying specific areas of concern.

Once all the data is collected, it should be reviewed by an assessment team. This team should comprise key stakeholders within the identified areas of risk, along with security and senior administrative personnel. The purpose of the team is to review the data and develop recommendations to improve the overall quality of the security program. Important to the metrics-based assessment is the implementation of recommended solutions. Data acts as a baseline in determining the effectiveness of resolutions and proven quality improvement metrics for the security program, which is a language that is better understood by the C-suite and senior management. Are you more likely to obtain $20,000 for a visitor management system for woman's health by presenting senior management with an anecdotal statement that your staff feels insecure or by presenting empirical data that includes incident reports, calls for response, and industry guidelines that document the risk of unauthorized visitors entering the maternity unit? Additionally, monies allocated to the visitor management project can be further justified by trending its long-term effectiveness through lower incident and call rates documented over time.

To conduct a thorough and complete assessment, major resources must be committed to the project over a long period of time. Because of this required commitment, consideration should be given to utilizing a third-party provider/consultant who understands the metrics-based assessment process. Working as a team, data collection and analysis can be conducted by the consultant, while recommendations can be developed through the in-house assessment team, leaving the security director to focus on appropriate resolutions. Recommendations determined by the assessment team can then be documented by the consultant and given to the security department to present to the C-suite. Follow-up can also be conducted by the consultant, providing trended data to the security director that demonstrates quality improvement to the security program over time.[1]

Reference

1. Scaglione, Bernard J. and Anthony J. Luizzo. Resources available for applying metrics in security and safety programming. *Journal of Healthcare Protection Management*, Vol. 32, No. 1, 27–33, 2017.

Appendix 1: Sample Facility Information Security Plan

Facility Information Security Plan

Policy

Hospital protects all Electronic Personal Health Information (EPHI) and its systems, the confidentiality, integrity, and availability of these, as well as the facilities in which they are located. *Hospital* prevents unauthorized access, tampering, and theft, ensuring that the level of security protection provided is commensurate with that of the identified threats and risks, documenting procedures that allow authorized workforce members entry to facilities based on their roles or functions or during a disaster, repair and modify physical components of the facilities that relate to security, providing appropriate authentication methods to take reasonable steps to ensure that only properly authenticated workforce members obtain access.

Procedure

Facility Access Control

Hospital limits physical access to EPHI systems and the facilities in which they are located, while taking reasonable steps to ensure that *Hospital* workforce members who are properly authorized have access to such EPHI systems and facilities, physically locates EPHI systems in locations where physical access can be controlled in order to minimize the risk of unauthorized access, takes reasonable steps to ensure that the level of protection provided for the EPHI systems, as well as the facilities in which they are housed, is commensurate with the threat of the identified threats and risks.

a. Ensure that the perimeter of facilities systems is physically sound, the external walls are properly constructed, and the external doors have the appropriate protections against unauthorized access.
b. Physical barriers used to protect against unauthorized entry are extended from the actual floor to the actual ceiling to prevent unauthorized access. Doors and windows of all facilities are locked when unattended. External protections, such as window guards or bars are installed on all windows at ground level and any other windows as reasonably necessary to prevent unauthorized entry.
c. The following controls are used at delivery and loading areas to prevent unauthorized access to its facilities:
   – Restrict access to a holding area from outside the building to identified and authorized workforce members.
   – Design the holding area so supplies can be unloaded without delivery staff gaining access to other areas of the building.
   – Secure the external doors of the holding area when the internal door of the area is open.
d. Ensure the level of protection provided for Electronic Information Systems, as well as the facilities in which they are housed, is commensurate with that of the identified threats and risks to these areas. A periodic risk analysis is performed in order to assess the level of physical access risk. The risk analysis results place areas in *Hospital's* facilities that contain Electronic Information Systems into documented categories:
   – Highly Sensitive – Areas where highly sensitive EPHI is created, received, transmitted, or maintained but only a small, select group of workforces need access to complete their job duties (e.g., data center, network closet, etc.).
   – Sensitive – Areas where sensitive EPHI is created, received, transmitted, or maintained and a moderately sized group of workforces need access to complete their job duties (e.g., radiology reading room, medical records department, etc.).
   – Monitoring Required – Areas where large amounts of EPHI are created, received, transmitted or maintained but a large group of workforces need access to complete their job duties (e.g., inpatient unit, outpatient clinic, public areas such as waiting room, etc.)

e. The Information Technology Department determines which workforce members are granted physical access rights to specific areas where Electronic Information Systems are maintained. Physical access rights are provided to workforce members having a need for access to such an area in order to complete job responsibilities.

f. The Information Technology Department reviews and revises physical access rights to *Hospital* areas are maintained on an ongoing basis.

g. Workforce members are required to visibly wear identification badges. Workforce members are required to report unescorted strangers or anyone not wearing visible identification to the Security Department.

h. All visitors are required to show proper identification and to sign in prior to gaining physical access to *Hospital* areas where Electronic Information Systems are located.

i. The Security Department conducts a periodic inventory of physical access controls used at its facilities to protect Electronic Information Systems.

Facility Security Plan

The facility security plan details how it protects facilities Electronic Information Systems from unauthorized access, tampering or theft. The facility security plan includes appropriate physical safeguards for Electronic Information Systems. The plan is reviewed and revised on a periodic basis.

a. A risk analysis is performed periodically as documented in the Risk Analysis policy, in order to assess the level of risk to facilities Electronic Information Systems. This risk analysis is the basis for the facility security plan.

b. *Hospital's* facility security plan addresses the following:
   - Identification of Electronic Information Systems to be protected from unauthorized access, tampering, or theft.
   - Identification of processes and controls used to protect Electronic Information Systems from unauthorized access, tampering, or theft.
   - Action to be taken if unauthorized access, tampering, or theft attempts have been made against Electronic Information Systems.
   - Identification of *Hospital's* workforce members' responsibilities within the facility security plan.

- Notification and reporting procedures.
- Maintenance schedule that specifies how and when the plan will be tested and a process for maintaining the facility security plan. *Hospital's* Security Officer is responsible for taking reasonable steps to ensure the plan is tested and maintained appropriately.

c. *Hospital* distributes the facility security plan to the necessary workforce members and an appropriate number of copies of the facility security plan are maintained off-site.

Access Control and Validation Procedures

Hospital determines and documents the level of sensitivity of each workplace area due to the nature of the information that is stored or available in such an area. The sensitivity of it is determined through risk analysis that is conducted periodically. *Hospital's* risk analysis will define levels of sensitivity assigned including areas deemed highly sensitive, sensitive and where monitoring is required.

a. *Hospital* proves workforce members limited access rights to highly sensitive areas only as needed in order to accomplish a legitimate business task.

b. *Hospital* defines and documents roles or functions that require physical access rights to highly sensitive areas.

c. *Hospital* reviews and, on a periodic basis, revises access rights to facilities and Electronic Information Systems as needed.

d. *Hospital* tracks and logs physical access to highly sensitive facilities. *Hospital* maintains the tracked and logged information in a secure manner. Such tracking and logging provide:
- Date and time of access
- Name or user ID of workforce member gaining access
- Name of workforce member that granted the access

e. *Hospital* instructs workforce members not to attempt to gain physical access to sensitive facilities containing Electronic Information Systems for which they have not been given proper authorization to access.

f. Workforce members are instructed to immediately report to the Security Department the loss or theft of any device (e.g., card or token) that enables them to gain physical access to sensitive facilities.

g. Workforce members are instructed to wear an identification badge when at facilities containing Electronic Information Systems. Workforce members are required to report unknown persons not wearing an identification badge.

h. Visitors to sensitive facilities are asked to show proper identification, state their reasons for needed access and sign in prior to gaining access.

Maintenance Records

a. *Hospital* conducts a periodic inventory of the physical components at its facilities that are related to physical security. Physical components related to security include:
   - Walls
   - Doors
   - Locks
   - Physical access, Electronic Information, Electronic Information Systems (e.g., card, keypad, biometric)

b. *Hospital's* documentation that describes the repairs and modifications made to the physical security components includes:
   - Date and time of repair or modification
   - Description of physical component prior to repair or modification
   - Reasons(s) for repair or modification, including any damage and any related security incident.
   - Person(s) performing repair or modification
   - Outcome of repair or modification

c. *Hospital* stores the documentation of the repairs and modifications to the physical security components, and the results of the periodic inventory, in a secure manner.

d. *Hospitals* that share or lease office space receive copies of repairs from the shared entity or lessee or require the shared entity or lessee to keep a copy of the repairs in order to make them available upon request.

e. *Hospital* provides training to the building maintenance personnel and any third-party vendors regarding the *Maintenance Records Policy* in order to take reasonable steps to ensure the (Security or other designated workforce member) is informed when a repair or modification is made that affect the physical security of *Hospital* facilities.

Contingency Operations

Hospital takes reasonable steps to ensure that in the event of a disaster or emergency, appropriate workforce members can enter its facilities to take the necessary actions as documented in its Disaster Recovery Plan policy and EOP policy.

Based on its disaster recovery plan, *Hospital* develops, implements, and periodically reviews a documented procedure to allow authorized workforce members access to *Hospital's* facilities to support restoration of lost data. *Hospital* defines workforce members' role in its disaster recovery plan, and addresses facilities, Electronic Information, Electronic Information Systems, and electronic media involved. "Electronic Information Systems" means *Hospital's* information, Electronic Information, Electronic Information Systems, repositories and conduits that contain EPHI. *Hospital's* disaster recovery plan defines how the actions taken by such workforce members are tracked and logged, and how unauthorized accesses can be detected and prevented.

Hospital develops, implements, and periodically reviews a documented procedure to allow authorized workforce members to enter *Hospital's* facility to enable continuation of processes and controls that protect the confidentiality, integrity, and availability of data while operating in emergency mode. *Hospital* defines workforce members' roles in its emergency mode operations plan. *Hospital's* emergency mode operations plan defines how the action taken by such workforce members are tracked and logged, and how unauthorized access can be detected and prevented.

In the event of a disaster or other emergency, only authorized *Hospital* workforce members are permitted to administer or modify processes and controls that protect the security of information. *Hospital's* emergency mode operations plan defines such workforce members and roles.

Person or Entity Authentication

a. *Hospital* maintains a documented authentication process for verifying the identity of any person or entity prior to granting them access to the organization. The process is reviewed and revised on a periodic basis by its Security Department.

b. *Hospital's* authentication process includes:
  – Documented procedure for granting persons and entities authentication credentials (e.g., password, token, digital signature, biometrics) or changing an existing authentication method.
  – Uniquely identifiable authentication identifiers in order to track the identifier to a workforce member.
  – Documented procedure for detecting and responding to any person or entity attempting to access without proper authentication.
c. *Hospital* uses an appropriate authentication method to take reasonable steps to ensure that only properly authenticated and authorized person or entities access. Appropriate access methods may include:
  – Unique user identifiers (user IDs)
  – Security identifier (password)
  – Password Electronic Information Electronic Information Systems
  – Personal Identification Number (PIN) Electronic Information Electronic Information System.
  – Security token Electronic Information Electronic Information Systems
  – Biometric identification Electronic Information Electronic Information Systems
  – Telephone callback Electronic Information Electronic Information Systems
  – Digital signatures
d. *Hospital* immediately removes or disables authentication credentials for persons or entities that no longer require access.
e. *Hospital* periodically validates that no redundant authentication credentials have been issued or are in use.
f. *Hospital's* Security Officer takes reasonable steps to ensure that workforce members are provided training and awareness about the authentication methods used by *Hospital.*
g. *Hospital* protects authentication credentials (e.g., passwords, PINs) with appropriate controls to prevent unauthorized access.
h. (When feasible) *Hospital's* authentication credentials mask, suppress, or otherwise obscure the passwords and PINs of persons and entities seeking to access so that unauthorized persons are not able to observe them.
i. Access methods for authentication to Electronic Information or Electronic Information Systems are not built into logon scripts. *Hospital's* Security Officer may make exceptions only after review and approval.

j. *Hospital* workforce members do not share or reveal their authentication methods to other workforce members.

k. *Hospital* workforce members are trained to report the loss due to theft of an access method (e.g., key card, security token) to their appropriate management.

l. *Hospital* workforce members activate their workstation locking software when they leave their workstation unattended for (time to be determined by covered entity) minutes. Locking software for unattended laptops is activated after (time to be entered by covered entity) minutes.

m. *Hospital* limits authentication attempts to no more than (covered entity to determine number of attempts) unsuccessful attempts in (covered entity to determine period) minutes. Authentication attempts that exceed the limit result in:
   – Relevant account being disabled for an appropriate period of time
   – Logging of event
   – Notification to appropriate *Hospital* management.

Responsibility: Security and Information Systems Department

References

Health Insurance Portability and Accounting Act of 1966, 45 CFR 164.312 (d)

Health Insurance Portability and Accounting Act of 1966, 45 CFR 164.310(a) (1)

Health Insurance Portability and Accounting Act of 1966, 45 CFR 164.310(a) (2) (ii)

Health Insurance Portability and Accounting Act of 1996, 45 CFR 164.310(1) (2) (iii)

Health Insurance Portability and Accounting Act of 1996, 45 CFR 164.310(1) (2) (iii)

Health Insurance Portability and Accounting Act of 1996, 45 CCFR 1643.310(1) (2) (iv)

Appendix 2: Sample Hospital Security Survey Schedule

Hospital Survey Schedule

- Physical tour of the property line and parking lots
- Physical tour of the exterior of all buildings including all entry and exit portals, windows, etc.
- Inside tour of all egress portals
- Inside tour of all facilities
- Focus on high risk areas:
  - Operating Rooms
  - Maternity
  - Pediatrics
  - Pharmacies
  - Behavioral Health
  - Cashier
  - Storerooms
  - Emergency Department
  - Dietary
  - Central Supply
  - Central Sterile Supply
  - Loading Dock
- Review of electronic security systems to include: alarm points, CCTV installations, card reader installations, guard tour system
- Exterior survey at night of lighting around parking areas and property and entry points
- List of Documents to review:
  - Staffing

- – Security Officer Schedule
- – Security Department Policies and Procedures
- – Security Post Locations and Hours
- – Security Management Plan
- – Job Descriptions of all job levels
- – Job Requirements of all job levels
- – Orientation Schedule or List of Activities
- ■ Training
  - – Training Outline
  - – Training Competencies
- ■ Hospital Policies Related to:
  - – Disaster Preparedness
  - – Infant/Child Abduction
  - – Identification
  - – Patient Elopement
  - – VIP
  - – Demonstration
  - – Workplace Violence
  - – Active Shooter
  - – Patient Valuables Policy
  - – Visitor Policy
  - – Behavioral Health/Restraint
  - – Lost and Found Policy
  - – Storage of Lost and Found policy
  - – Any cash handling policy
  - – Access control/badging for vendors
  - – Smoking/non-smoking on campus
  - – Handling of violent or disruptive patients
- ■ Performance improvement indicators for 2016
- ■ Yearly EOC review
- ■ Reports
  - – Sample Incident Report
  - – Incident Report data for past three years
  - – EOC Reports for three years
  - – Any prior risk assessments
  - – Area crime survey
- ■ Technology
  - – Access control system locations and specifications
  - – CCTV system specifications and locations

- Security/CCTV company contracts and PM agreements
- Duress or panic button specifications and locations
- Key Control policies and procedures
■ Other Considerations
- List of all Entrances and Exits
- List of Security Sensitive areas
- Fire protection and fire/smoke detector locations
- Pharmacy and locations within hospital
- ATMs on-site, locations and controls

Appendix 3: Sample New Employee Orientation Program

Day One

1130 – 1200 – New Security Officers are welcomed to the Security Department. Arrangements for the acquisition of uniforms are made.

1200 – 1300 – Lunch

1300 – 1400 – Supervisor's Patrol

The training officers are taken on a patrol with their training supervisor and shown each post. Specific procedures of each post are explained and reviewed by the training supervisor as well as the security officers on the posts. They are shown the hospital, college, and surrounding property and grounds. Vital areas of the property are empathized and fully explained. All of the hospital and college patrols are explained and a list of them is given and reviewed. Safety and Emergency Room Policy/Procedure are explained and reviewed.

1400 – 1500 – Operations and Command Room

The Officers then take a tour of the Command Room and Identification Unit. Each officer spends an amount of allotted time becoming aware of the operations of each area. Operation procedures are explained and reviewed by the command room personnel. Fire safety procedures are handed out and reviewed.

1500 – 1600 –Training Film – "Orientation to Security"

The Security Department Instructional handbook is handed out and reviewed. Instructional video is shown, questioned, and reviewed by training supervisor and/or Security Manager. The trainees are prepped for their second day of orientation.

Day Two

0800 – 0945 – Training – Customer Service

Trainees are shown instructional video. Video contains information and directions on how a security officer should perform with a courteous attitude while trying to enforce hospital policy and procedure. At completion of video they are tested and have opportunity to ask questions based on the video. The questions are reviewed, as are the test results.

0945 – 1100 – Training – Crisis Intervention

Video is shown containing vital information and specific instructions on how to put an end to aggression using calming methods. The video is reviewed and the training supervisor performs a question and answer forum with the training officers.

1100 – 1200 – Lunch

1200 – 1330 – Fire Response and Control

Trainees are shown video containing procedures regarding Fire Safety and Precautions in case of a Fire. Video goes in depth to show every situation that could possibly arise from a fire. The Security Officers play a vital part of the Fire Safety Policy and all actions taken by the security personnel are reviewed and tested.

1330 – 1500 – Disaster Response

Video is shown highlighting the role that a security officer embarks on during a disaster. The video also shows various situations that could be regarded as disasters and what actions a security guard should perform during these times.

Contents of the video are tested and reviewed.

1500 – 1600 – Policy and Procedure Review

All contents of each video are reviewed. Fire safety policy and procedure are reviewed in conjunction with all policies and procedures that the videos explain. Training Supervisor performs a review of all material that is taught, and a final question and answer forum is conducted. The trainees are prepped for their third day of orientation.

Day Three

0800 – 1100 – Post Training
All posts are covered and the officers are trained by a senior officer on all post procedures and policy. Customer Service policy is explained and reviewed.

1100 – 1200 – Lunch

1200 – 1600 – Post Training
Post training procedures and policy for the hospital and college positions are explained to trainees.

Day Four

0800 – 1200 – Review and Testing
All subject matters are reviewed and tested.
Videos, booklets, and policy and procedures are reviewed in detail.

1200 – 1300 – Lunch

1300 – 1600 – Question and Answer Forum
Trainees are given a final question and answer session where all answers are reviewed.

Appendix 4: Sample New Employee Orientation Check List

Employee Name: ___ Date Completed: ___

Completed by: _____

Administrative

- ☐ Personal Information Received
- ☐ Licensing Paperwork Completed
- ☐ Uniforms and Equipment Assigned
- ☐ Locker Assigned

Tours

- ☐ Tour of the Hospital, College and Surrounding Property and Grounds
- ☐ Tour of Each Post
- ☐ Tour of the Command Room
- ☐ Tour of Identification Unit
- ☐ Tour of All Hospital and College Patrols

Policy and Procedure

- ☐ The Security Department Instructional Handbook Handed Out and Review
- ☐ Post Procedures Review

- [ ] Fire Safety and Emergency Policy/Procedure Review
- [ ] Customer Service Policy Review
- [ ] Final Review of Videos, Booklets, Policy and Procedures

Films

- [ ] "Orientation to Security"
- [ ] "Courteous Enforcement"
- [ ] "Calming the Aggressor"
- [ ] "Fire Response and Control"
- [ ] "Disaster Response"

On-The-Job Training

- [ ] Trained by Senior Officers on All Posts

Licensing Requirements

- [ ] Issued the Security Guard Act 16 Hour On-the-Job Training Exam

Appendix 5: Sample Training Policy

XXXX Hospital

Policy: XXXX Hospital educates and trains all security staff during orientation and annually in order to provide security staff with information to provide a safe and secure environment for all patients, visitors and hospital staff.

Purpose: A training program has been developed and implemented to provide training for all security staff on a regular and consistent basis.

To gain an understanding of the basic concepts and methods in security services management and have detailed knowledge of all policies and procedures, process and job functions required to provide a safe and secure environment for all patients, visitors, and staff.

Procedure: Security staff will be trained through the use of classroom learning which will require all new employees and existing employees, annually, to participate in all classroom training session provided by the Security Department and hospital.

Learning Objectives

By the end of training sessions, participants will:

1. Demonstrate knowledge of key concepts and principles for posts assignments, job functions, and all department and hospital policies and procedures.
2. Understand how to provide customer service when carrying out officer and supervisory duties.

3. Know how to respond to all emergent situations and provide a safe and secure environment for all patients, visitors, and staff. What a pitiful thing to
4. Have detailed knowledge of all hospital locations, hours of operations and be able to provide directions and office hours to all persons entering the hospital or needing wayfinding assistance.

Standards

All security staff will learn Department policies and procedures along with all hospital policies that pertain to the security of the hospital. All job functions required for each position within the Security Department will be reviewed and all hospital locations and hours of operations will be reviewed with each staff member. All participants are required to attend the classroom sessions and participate in classroom activities.

Measurement

All training sessions will be required to have a pre and posttest in order to determine the level of competency of each officer attending the training sessions. Each posttest will have a minimum passing grade of 70%.

Annual Evaluation

All training programs and sessions will be evaluated annually to determine their effectiveness in providing staff with the knowledge necessary to carry out their job functions. Annual evaluation will include:

- Student class evaluations
- Competency grades
- Review of course content
- Instructor evaluations

Index